Bringing Up BRITS

Expat parents raising
cross-cultural kids in Britain

Meghan Peterson Fenn

lịp

First published in 2011 by:

Live It Publishing
27 Old Gloucester Road, London,
United Kingdom, WC1N 3AX.
www.liveitpublishing.com

ISBN 978-1-906954-21-5 (pbk)

For my children, Samuel, Anna Grace and Jonah
And for my husband, Nick

This book is dedicated to my parents,
Doug and Joanne Peterson
Thank you for choosing me

Acknowledgements

Thank you to my contributors and those who helped me find contributors and for all your encouragement and support: Noriko, Arianna, Grazyna, Ania, Mollie, Larry, Assia, Nining, Fabio, Ahlam, Charlotte, Estera, Linda, Melissa, Emilie, Mi, Anne, Heidi, Sari, Julia, Andreas, Aja, Tiffiney, Soila, Murielle, Joyce, Suzanne, Chris, Eileen, Sarah, Jane, Debbie, Ruth, Moose, Antonia, Sara and Helen.

Contents

Introduction

Why did this book need to be written? What does this book do, and who are the parents behind it?

There are a few answers, really, to the first question posed in this chapter's title "Why did this book need to be written?" As an expat parent raising British children in Britain, I am not alone. Births to mothers born outside the United Kingdom accounted for 24.7% of all live births in 2009[1]. That's nearly a quarter of all live births in Britain! Surely, as expat parents, we share some common experiences. I wanted to find out more about what those common experiences were.

Another reason is quite simply that I've always wanted to write a book and for a long time I had been thinking about writing about my experience as an American living in England and raising British children. I wasn't sure if it was a worthwhile pursuit until I met Antonia Chitty, a fellow Mumpreneur and author of *The Mumpreneur Guide*[2], who convincingly encouraged me to actually do it. In addition, I thought it was high time I did something for myself, something that didn't revolve around the school run or nappy changes or buying groceries. I'd been inspired by one of my clients, another fellow Mumpreneur, Melissa Talago, who sailed the first leg of the *Clipper Round the World Race*. She took part in this race for herself – to do something completely different to her everyday life of raising children and running a business. Like Melissa, I wanted to do something inspiring and interesting to engage with something that wasn't mum related or anything to do with running my two businesses, *White Ochre Design*, and my informational website for families, *Better Days Out*. I feel I have achieved that by writing this book and in the process have surprisingly discovered in a very positive way, that it has everything to do with being a mum to my children. And although I may not be from Britain, as a result of researching and writing this book, I have come to realise I am part of a very large community in the UK – that of expat parents who call Britain home for now and that has definitely helped me in my journey to find where I belong at this point in time in my life and I hope it does the same for others.

Another more complex answer is that I wanted to explore my relationship with my children and my English husband as an American 'Mom' raising English kids. I thought that the challenges we come across and the issues surrounding our family dynamic, as a result of two cultures coming together, needed to be discussed, to be

Introduction

studied, compared and documented somehow. We are part of what makes Britain, Britain today. I suppose it also stemmed from an innate desire as a mother, as a parent to record every little thing my children did and what we did together as a family. All those moments that every parent wants to wrap up and save. Like a phrase they use that's grammatically incorrect but expresses the meaning more clearly than if it were grammatically correct. The first time they challenge you and you realise they are actually really smart and maybe you don't have all the answers. This natural compulsion coupled with the dynamic of raising our family within a combination of both British and American cultures while living in Britain made it seem even more important and somehow more intriguing on a whole new level.

I also wanted to share my experiences with other non-British parents who were raising children here. What things did we have in common, what challenges did we share, and what other different issues did they have that our family did not experience? And finally, I wanted to create a legacy for my cross-cultural children, for their future and for their own children. It is this more complex answer that I want to explore in more depth and to share with you.

To answer the second question, "What does this book do?" I think it does several things. First and foremost, it is a triangulation of my and other parents' experiences. It illustrates common ideas, themes and truths. It shows a connection we have to other parents who are also raising cross-cultural kids. It is a source of comfort, support and inspiration for other non-British parents. It is an interesting read (I hope!), mildly controversial and provides an insight into raising children in Britain. Before having children, I would have gratefully read a book like this book, and since having had children, I would be even more interested in reading a book like this! Anne, a French mum with two children living in Glasgow commented, "It's a great idea for a book and I'd be happy to contribute in any way I can. I would really look forward to reading it as well. There are so many aspects that are still very much question marks for me". An English friend and mum told me, "What a great idea – I know so many parents who would love to read your book, and I would love to read it too!"

Before moving to England, having read *Notes From a Small Island*[3] by Bill Bryson, and having had parents who lived in Cambridge, England during the first few years of their marriage, I had a somewhat vague idea but completely biased view of what Britain would be like. Some things I expected, like not having a dishwasher, calling cookies 'biscuits', and not getting a side salad with my main meal as standard. Although once I had physically settled here – bought the house, got the job, had the

Introduction

child – I still felt like an outsider looking in, always two steps behind other English parents purely because I was trying to figure out what words like 'consultant' and 'reception' actually meant as opposed to what I thought they might mean. I was still confused, still unsure and very much wanted to fit in and do the right sort of mum things for my children whilst retaining some of my own 'American-ness' and instilling in them a sense of American culture. From interviewing other parents of other nationalities, it is clear there are parents for whom this sentiment also rings true. It is certain that we share the commonality of raising cross-cultural kids and the practical and emotional challenges that are inherent in this. This book is THE book to read if you are a non-British parent (or if you grew up in a different country and are) raising your children in Britain, and in addition if you have family or friends who are touched by this.

Secondly and more personally, writing it has been a cathartic experience. The decision to live here and raise our children here wasn't openly stated between myself and my husband nor did I think much of it at the time. Emotionally it has always been difficult but I never considered that to be of particular importance. I now realise that is of great importance and hugely influences how I raise my children. Furthermore, I'm not alone, there are thousands of other parents who have similar experiences and who struggle with the many issues

Bringing Up BRITS

surrounding the simple fact that their children are growing up in a country foreign to them.

The parents who have contributed to this book are from neighbouring countries such as France, Germany and Italy as well as from far reaching countries such as Canada, Australia, China and Japan. I've heard stories from parents from Poland, The Emirates and Indonesia. I and the many parents who have contributed to this book, parents who are from all over the world, have a common link. We are all raising our children here in Britain, a place foreign to us and one in which we ourselves did not grow up in. We share an emotional experience regardless of where we originally come from and regardless of the details. Some of the parents who've contributed to this book are married to or have partners who are British. Other parents have partners who are also non-British. Some have lived here for 10 years, some for 2. I've included a list of parents to illustrate (as well as to credit them) how significant, current and relevant this book is.

- Noriko – Japanese raising 2 children in England, Iranian husband

- Arianna – Canadian raising 1 child in England, English husband

- Grazyna – Polish raising 1 child in England, English husband

- Larry – American, raising 2 children in England, English wife

Introduction

- Mollie – American raising 4 children in England, English husband

- Assia – French Algerian raising 3 children in Scotland, French/Columbian husband

- Fabio – Italian raising 3 children in England, English wife

- Claudia – German raising 2 children in England, German husband

- Ahlam – Emirati raising 3 children in England, English husband

- Charlotte – French raising 1 child in Glasgow, Scottish partner

- Nining – Indonesian rasing 2 children in England, English husband

- Estera – Romanian raising 1 child in England, English husband

- Linda – Chinese raising 2 children in England, English husband

- Emilie – French raising 1 child in Scotland, English husband

- Melissa – American raising 2 children in England, English husband

- Anne – French raising 2 children in Scotland, English husband

- Heidi – American raising 3 children in England (currently living in China), English husband

- Sari – Indonesian raising 2 children in England, English husband

Bringing Up BRITS

- Julia – German raising 1 child in England, English husband

- Andreas – Sweden raising 2 children in England, Swiss/British wife

- Tiffiney – Australian raising 1 child in England, English husband

- Mi – Swedish raising 1 child in England, English husband

- Aja – British/Slovakian raising 2 children in England, English husband

- Soila – British/Kenyan raising 2 children in England, Danish husband

- Eileen – British mother of 3, Australian husband

Introduction

Babies to foreign mothers at record levels

By Tom Whitehead, Home Affairs Editor,
The Telegraph, 7:00AM BST 27 Aug 2010

The proportion of babies born to foreign mothers is at a record high, with migrants accounting for three quarters of births in some parts of the country.

One in four births in England and Wales last year were to a mother born overseas, according to the Office for National Statistics.

They accounted for 174,174 births, representing 24.7 per cent of the 706,248 new arrivals in 2009.

That was the highest proportion since the nationality of mothers started being recorded in 1969 and has doubled in the last 20 years alone.

Chapter 1

Finding Identity: Who am I?
Making your Mark and Creating a Home

I was born in Seoul, Korea and never knew my birth mother or my biological father. At 8 months, whilst living in a Korean orphanage just outside of Seoul, I was adopted by American parents (actually an American father and a Canadian mother at the time) and brought to Massachusetts USA where I instantly became the first daughter and a little sister in a brand new family. I grew up in two different states in New England, then in Texas and finally in Tennessee. I grew up as an American girl although I looked oriental. At age 6 I went through the US naturalisation process and formally became an American citizen. I was raised on American food, spoke only American English and grew up with the same American traditions, dreams and work ethics that everyone else in our world had. I was a typical American kid and did typical American kid things – went to church, went to summer camp, hung out at the mall, at age 16 got my driver's licence, played hooky from school, got a part-time job as a busgirl (clearing tables in a restaurant, a rite

Finding Identity

of passage for many American teens), and ceremoniously graduated from high school.

After this I went to College (University) in Virginia, spent half my Junior year abroad in Italy, and got my degree in English Creative Writing with a minor in Fine Art. I then left the States to teach English as a Foreign Language at the University of Prague in the Czech Republic. This was the turning point in my life and where it changed forever. For it was in an over-heated, over-crowded British expat bar in Prague that I met the most inebriated and most incredibly fascinating person I'd ever seen, up to that point, who eventually became my husband and the father of my half British children. We immediately became a couple (in so much as you *could* be a couple in bohemian Prague in 1994!) and continued to live and work in Prague for two years. We then moved to Tokyo, after spending an abruptly short time in England (I hated it and refused to stay the first time round!), and taught English to Japanese salary men, office ladies and charming school girls and boys for two and a half years. Christmas 1999, we finally took the plunge and moved to Nottingham England where I embarked on a Masters degree at the Nottingham Trent University. Nick and I got married in his home town of Telford, in the Midlands and started to make a life together in Britain. A year later, in 2001, our first child Samuel was born, followed by Anna Grace in 2003 and Jonah who was born in 2009.

Bringing Up BRITS

Re-locating to a foreign country can be a big move. When I first moved to Prague from the States it was like stepping into the unknown. Aside from not knowing anybody in Prague, I really knew nothing about living outside the US. But, that actually didn't matter – I was young, looking for adventure and single! Plus, I just assumed I'd return in a few years' time to go to graduate school or land that perfect job. So, when I moved to England I underestimated just how much of a BIG move it was. Since I had already been living abroad for 5 years, it didn't seem too daunting a prospect. In fact, it almost seemed like coming 'home', moving back West after living in Tokyo, a far Eastern culture even more foreign than Prague. On the surface, it seemed completely practical and natural. After all, England wasn't too different to the US, people spoke English, ate regular carb-based foods and slept in normal beds. So it was true, it wasn't as foreign as Tokyo. However, in a way, that made it even more difficult to acclimatise. I felt I was *supposed* to be able to fit in automatically and naturally. I didn't. Nick, on the other hand, was home. This was his birthplace, his country and his people. Not only did I look foreign (ironically, unlike in Tokyo), but I felt foreign too. I was utterly surprised at my lack of being able to fit in and I had a great sense of loss of my own identity. It was difficult to talk to people in social situations because nobody seemed interested in talking to me. People were taken aback and sometimes even

Finding Identity

outraged if I spoke to them without an obvious reason. I was given the cold shoulder and grim, frowny expressions if I tried to make eye contact or even look like I was on the verge of speaking to someone next to me in line or waiting for a bus.

All this left me feeling completely at a loss, lonely and discouraged. My husband couldn't understand what I was going through – he'd come home and find me bawling over the sick and abandoned kittens being saved on *Pet Rescue*. To make matters worse, during my first six months in England, it rained so much I couldn't bear going out. I felt cheated and isolated, but most of all disappointed in myself. Living abroad is supposed to be exciting and offer unique and thrilling experiences. Despite my efforts, I couldn't get out of the funk I was in. For me, as an American living in central England, I was dying a slow death – all my energy was being sapped out and I felt powerless. It made me question what I thought I knew about social norms and etiquette. Was I shallow because I wanted to make small talk with a complete stranger just to be friendly? Was I not worthy to speak with? Is it wrong to want to make friends with people even though there might only be a small or even miniscule chance a friendship will blossom? Not knowing social etiquette whilst living in Prague and Tokyo didn't have this type of impact on me. It was OK not to know there – nobody knew! But here in England, that wasn't the case. It was like everyone was part of a special club and I wasn't allowed in or even to watch and try to learn what to do to become accepted. I also questioned my instincts and natural reaction to people and situations. For instance, my natural reaction to a problem would be to tackle it openly, with confidence that a solution could be found. This didn't seem to be the way things were done. Conversations that were supposed to be decision making would leave me feeling ambiguous, frustrated and confused. All of this contributed to an overwhelming feeling of insecurity and loneliness.

Nining, Indonesian mum of two British children also found it hard in the beginning:

> *"The first year was very difficult as I did not have any friends or family in this country. Family is very important and the closeness between family members. I didn't have that at all when I moved here."*

For Nining there was a major loss of family and the security that a family unit inherently provides. Because I had been living abroad and away from my family before moving to England, I didn't have such a strong sense of loss regarding family. For me, it was more like a void needing to be filled rather than a loss. True, if I had had the support of family members it would have made a

Finding Identity

difference, but I did not feel a loss in the same way as Nining. For many parents who are from cultures where families are close-knit, where children live with extended family or with their parents into adulthood, Nining's experience resonates. She says:

> "It took a while but I have made a lot of friends, most of them from my local mosque. They are not just friends but also a surrogate family."

She found a way to reclaim a sense of family and closeness which in turn helped her to deal with the loss of her biological family and provide her children with a similar upbringing amongst a close 'family'. By creating a surrogate family around her she is making a mark for herself and for her children, ensuring a secure home and future for them here in England.

It wasn't really until I had my first child that I began to 'break through', to gain confidence in myself and feel secure in my own identity again. Making friends was important and crucial to my survival, not only as a foreigner but as a new mother too. Heidi, an American mother of 3, married to an English man also found it easier to meet people post children. She says:

> "Definitely having children helped us to meet people in Teddington. We lived there for 3 years before

having children and we never became friends with anyone there. We finally met other people our same age once the kids started at a local nursery."

Julia, a German mother of one with one on the way comments:

"I didn't have many friends for a long time, nor did I know any neighbours, as I worked long hours in our own business. Only when I started to work part-time as a museum assistant, I made some friends at work. With the first baby, a whole new era started, I made lots of friends from my aqua-natal group, and from the weekly clinic/baby play group. These contacts have lasted until now, and probably will for a long time. We help each other, and since the clinic brings together women from the same neighbourhood, we all live close together, which makes meeting up easy."

I cannot stress enough: parents and parents to be – join an antenatal group and then once you've had your baby, join a baby and toddler group. These can be lifelines (obviously not just for foreign parents!) and can make a significant difference to your life. I eventually became the Chair of my local baby and toddler group and through this I made a life-long friend, met new people, gained a sense of purpose and felt proud that I was contributing to a

Finding Identity

community that was becoming 'my' community. For me, this new sense of belonging was my own lifeline and personal achievement.

Feeling a part of something, no matter how large or small, was the turning point in my new life in England and as a parent to a British child. I had worked very hard at it as well. It wasn't instant or easy – at this point I had been in Britain for just over 3 years! Despite hearing about all the wonderful friendships that can be formed through NCT antenatal groups, the antenatal course my husband and I attended was a disaster. Although everyone was polite and friendly, there was no scope for building friendships which was made only too clear to me at the 'reunion' after we had all had our babies. There I was thinking that because we had all shared this life-changing time together that we might want to keep in touch and maybe some of us would become friends, something at the time I was desperate for. That sounds sad and pitiful, but it was the truth. It turned out that nobody wanted to make the effort apart from us and therefore no numbers were exchanged, ensuring no further contact. My first venture out to a baby group, I felt shunned because nobody spoke to me. My second was at a bumps and babies gathering at a parent's house. It was like people were speaking a foreign language or part of an exclusive club, I had only just figured out what they were talking about when they had moved on to another topic altogether, leaving me mute and panicky. The next baby and parent gathering I attended went marginally better but most of the mums just looked quizzically at me whenever I opened my mouth. (It's starting to sound like something is wrong with me! I assure you I am a normal person – just foreign.)

So, yes it took a while, but determination coupled with the need for an outlet for my growing toddler meant that I stuck it out and made a success of it in the end with the toddler group I became part of. That gave me the confidence I needed and in turn, helped me to adapt to a life in England. It was all part of the process of learning how to be accepted and finding my place and my own identity as a non-British mother in a British world. I think for me it was doubly challenging because although I looked foreign and non-English, I didn't look American. I wasn't actually what I looked like, ie., Chinese or Japanese which was what most people assumed I was. So there was an additional layer of misunderstanding that people found difficult to see through and I found it difficult to remember that the perceptions people had of me were completely different to my own perception of myself as a non-Brit. Ultimately, the baby and toddler group that I became so involved with was the catalyst for me being able to establish myself and create a place for myself.

Finding Identity

Sarah, mum of 3 and married to a German husband set up a German baby and toddler group which is open to anyone. She had lived in Germany where she met and married her husband and had their first two children. They then moved to England where they were faced with the challenge of bringing up their dual nationality and bilingual children in Britain. By setting up this group, Sarah created a supportive and familiar place for her husband, for their children and for other parents in similar circumstances. Noriko, a Japanese mum of 2 runs a Japanese community baby & toddler group for Japanese parents. Parents can come to these groups and speak their native language, swap stories and expose their bilingual (or more) children to their own cultures. At the end of this book there is a list of useful resources for finding local baby and toddler groups. These groups offer support and practical resources for parents from non-English speaking countries bringing up their children in Britain. Assia, a French mum of 3 contributes:

> "At the beginning, it was very hard because of the language barrier and my son was just 2 months old at that time. Things got better when he started to go to nursery and attend different activities. I started to get to know people and meet up with them outside."

Starting from scratch in a new country is daunting and these types of groups are vital in helping parents like myself and Assia find security, familiarity and create and nurture a sense of home.

Looking back, the memories of my first few years in England are still vivid. There might always be a lingering sense of isolation as an American living in Britain, but this is partially inherent. And I have mellowed significantly. I believe I have gained an insight into the British psyche and the paranoia that is so common and which left me feeling so misunderstood. It still does occasionally but through experience, I am better equipped to deal with it and it's now only a minor annoyance which does not cause the level of stress that it had before. I also believe that although I am still adapting, in many ways, I have found my place in England. This is mainly due to having my children and in part through my career. Of course there will always be an element of change and change is fluid, but with my children and through my children I feel a sense of home. I think this is very difficult. Grazyna, Polish mum married to an English husband says:

"I still have not found my place here yet."

Grazyna has been living and raising her daughter here in England since 2002. Emilie, a French mum to one comments:

Finding Identity

"Over the years, I have lost a lot of my own cultural identity."

I, for one, can empathise with Emilie. Although I feel 'at home' here and for the most part feel I have found my place in Britain, I am travelling further and further away from my American identity. I do not feel British, but my own cultural identity is becoming increasingly fainter.

For some, finding their place and feeling at home may come more easily. Mollie, mum of 4 and married to an Englishman says:

"I didn't feel isolated. I have a very close relationship with my husband's family who are very supportive in many ways. All the English family celebrate my American qualities and quirks! My ante-natal group says they won't let me ever leave!!!"

I'm sure everyone will have different experiences due to their own circumstances but there is a common thread that links all parents who have moved here from other countries and who are raising their children here. We did not grow up in Britain yet we re-located here and are raising our children in a British society. For me, finding and nurturing my own identity as an American mother is an important part of bringing up my British children in Britain.

Funny story

My first son's name is Sam. At a toddler group another mum asked me what my toddler's name was and I replied "Sam". I guess my accent made it sound like "Sayam" so she said, "Sayam?" and I said no, "Sam". Then she introduced me to her friend saying, "this is Meghan and her son Sayam". All I could do was smile obligingly.

Finding Identity

Funny story

My daughter's name is Anna Grace. When I first came up with the name, Nick was against it, saying English people don't use double-barrelled first names. They don't understand the concept, he told me. So, for the sake of my husband, she was actually born just Anna with one of her middle names being Grace. However, he would catch me calling her Anna Grace behind his back and to other people and when referring to her with other people. I think he realised that I was going to call her Anna Grace no matter what British people thought! So, she was re-christened Anna Grace. On several occasions the conversation about her name goes something like this:

Other mum: What's her name?

Me: Anna Grace

Other mum: Ella Grace?

Me: No, Anna Grace

Other mum: Emma Grace?

Me: No, Anna Grace

Other mum: Enna Grace

Me: No, Anna Grace

Other mum: Oh Emma Grace, that's a lovely name.

Chapter 2

**Isolation: The physicality of raising children
in a foreign land**

It depresses me when some mums tell me how close
their parents live to them or that they get a 'day off' once
a week because their mum will take the children. Those
mums tell me they would find it a real struggle if they
didn't have their own parents close by to help out. Even
for simple things like doctor's appointments or needing
someone to watch the kids whilst they pop out for an
hour to run an errand. Doing this errand with kids in tow
would be a total nightmare so being able to have your
mum pop over to stay with them would certainly be
easier. I know so many mums who get a whole weekend
away because they can drop their kids at their parents'
house and have a child-free weekend. It sounds
wonderful and I am insanely envious of this.

What's worse is when some mums complain about
having their parents or their in-laws as babysitters. I want
to slap them! When I exclaim to them how nice it would
be to have their parents look after their children so they

Isolation

could go out or have a weekend away, the response is hardly ever 'Yes, it's great!', it's normally, 'It is good, but.....' and then various reasons why it isn't so good for them. One mum even said how much of a pain it was to pack the bags for her children and said it almost wasn't worth it! Now that *is* like a slap in the face!

So what are the implications for parents raising their children in a foreign country, far away from their own parents and extended families? Ahlam is from the Emirates, she's a mum of 3 children all born in Britain and is married to an English man. She states:

"I don't have the help and support of the extended family. My sister gets lots of help from our mum and other members of our family. For me, it would be so much easier in a practical sense. I could leave my children with my mum and go do the shopping for example."

Ahlam comes from a society where extended family members live together or very close by and everyone is responsible for raising the children. Her sister doesn't even have to ask their mother to look after the children, it's part of their normal everyday life. Grazyna, Polish mum married to an English man says she has no feeling of security being so far away from her family:

Bringing Up BRITS

"In Poland I could phone my brother in the middle of the night if something happened he would be in my place in 5 minutes. I would never dream of even asking my in-laws to come over at such short notice. Once I really needed help and asked them but they refused because it wasn't planned."

It can be lonely and difficult being far from family whilst bringing up a young family. I think this is a real challenge for those parents who don't have their own family members and extended family close by.

Mi, a Swedish mum of one British born child comments:

"I find it difficult because of the lack of family around. I really wanted to build up a network of people I could rely on in support, but it's very disappointing how little people are there for you. I have to pay for almost all child care."

Soila, a British Kenyan mother of two who grew up in Kenya has lived in Britain for 20 years and holds a British passport. She says the hardest thing for her children growing up in Britain is being away from their Kenyan family. Soila says:

"Both my children look forward to going back to Kenya because they have lots of cousins to hang

around with. They have the outside space to play
around in too. Family. Family. Family."

Aja is originally from Slovakia and moved here when she
was 18. She, like Soila, holds a British passport. Aja is
married to a British man and has two British born
children. She says:

"I have got my own family unit now although I still
miss my family in Slovakia – I actually think the older
I am getting I miss them more and wish they could
have bigger part in my childrens lives."

Even though Soila and Aja are British, they were not born
here nor did they grow up in Britain. Both of their own
families are in their home countries so they do not have
them nearby.

Even those mums I know whose parents live far away but
still in England, they are still able to see them on a regular
basis, on main holidays like Christmas and Easter and for
birthdays and special occasions. There is a huge
difference between being a car journey away and an
airplane flight away. On the surface it might not sound so
far away – oh we can just hop on a plane! Well, it is
hopping on a plane with 3 young children, 3 lots of kids'
paraphanalia, full to bursting nappy bag, a whole case
dedicated to snacks, and the wholly unsuitable toys I said

no to that *had* to come along for the ride. And then it's 16 hours of travel, 16 tantrums and endless trips to the tiny unsanitary toilet. Just to be clear, I can confirm, it isn't as easy as it sounds, and I haven't even mentioned the cost element. Tiffiney, an Australian mum of one says:

> *"The hardest thing about raising my child here in Britain is being so far away from relatives at home. The thought of flying a 3 year old back to Oz fills me with fear!"*

Julia, a German mum of one and one on the way married to an English man, is able to go home more often simply because of the close proximity of her home country. Despite this, she says it is still the hardest thing about raising her children here in Britain. Julia says:

> *"The distance from my family and their whole way of life, including the language is the hardest part of raising my child here. We are flying to see them as often as we can, which is 2-3 times a year. At nearly 3, my son is a frequent flyer already!"*

I think there is also an element of psychological and emotional distance to cope with. While I am here in England, America seems soooo far away, we are on the other side of the world! The long distance is palpable, especially when I consider my children. How often do

Isolation

they see and spend time with their American grandparents? Their American Aunts and Uncles and cousins?

My in-laws moved to Spain when my older children were 6 and 5 so now we don't see them as often as we used to. Now it isn't an option to have them babysit for us. However, before our 3rd child, Jonah, was born when they were still living in England, they came and stayed at our house and looked after the children for us so we could go to Prague for our 10th anniversary weekend. This was gold for us and I can only imagine if it were still a possibility! How wonderful it would be to have that. Obviously my parents live in the States so we rely on friends to babysit or pay a sitter for an evening.

But seriously, it's not just about having babysitters on tap or being able to have endless child-free weekends. It's about knowing that your children will be safe, that they are with people who love them unconditionally and *most importantly* it's about the bond that forms between grandchildren and grandparents or with aunts, uncles and cousins that is so valuable and important.

Grandparents can become a real and constant part of a child's life. They form their own unique relationship with each other. This is something my children and parents do not have and in all likelihood will never have. At least my parents will never have that type of relationship whilst they are still young enough to experience them and enjoy them and my children won't spend time with their grandparents during their formative years. Being a part of their everyday life is not an option for them.

"The hardest thing about raising my children here in Britain is being so far away from my own family and all that encompasses."

This was the number 1 response from parents when I asked them what was difficult about bringing up their children here in Britain when they themselves are from other countries. It may be an obvious answer but the implications are huge for both the parents and their children.

For me, because I am so far away from everyone, it's difficult to feel supported by my parents, my brothers and my sisters. We don't see each other on a regular basis so my children can't form a close relationship with them. There is little opportunity to bond with my family. My children do not know their American aunts and uncles nor do they know their American cousins. This is sad for me and disappointing for my children. My older two have met their American aunts and uncles only once and my 3rd has not met them yet. The brief time they have spent with them was wonderful and I kept wishing we were

Isolation

able to meet up more often. But the reality of it is that it isn't affordable nor is it practical in terms of school holidays and the amount of time off work required to make such expensive trips. My 3rd child hasn't even met my father yet, although remarkably, we were able to video Skype just after he was born. My father couldn't be with us in person, but he was able to see his newborn grandson just a few days after he was born.

For me, one of the hardest aspects about being so far away from my family is that I am not close with my younger sister and her children. I do not know her children and I cannot spend time with them as their aunty. I feel guilty that I wasn't there when she became a mother for the first time, not being able to support her by physically being there. Yes, I could send her letters giving her an insight into what it's like to become a mother and yes I could send her books that she might find useful, but not being able to be there to laugh, cry and support each other is something I'll always feel bad about for both of us.

I think guilt is a significant part of the difficulty of being so far away from our families. And feeling guilty is lonely and isolating because no one understands it. My husband understands why I feel guilty, but it's not his guilt so he doesn't have to live with it. My in-laws can't relate to it because they are not in my situation so how could they possibly. We just say, 'well, that's just the way it is and we have to deal with it'. Yes of course, OK. But that doesn't make it any easier or less of an emotional struggle. Mollie, an American mother of 4 says:

> *"I do feel like I have hurt my parents by not being close by to share my children and their lives with them."*

This resonates with me so much. I can audibly hear the pain in my mother's voice when she comments on how fast the children are growing up and how much Jonah has changed since he was born. She wants to be a part of their lives. Most importantly perhaps, my children want their grandparents to be part of their lives. I often talk about my family, we have lots of pictures and we talk about the trip we had to America (the one they can remember). The Internet is a fantastic tool for keeping in touch. We Skype and email my family as I'm sure many other parents in my situation do with their families. Nining, mum of two children born here in Britain, uses Facebook to keep in contact with her family in Indonesia. She says:

> *"I miss my family. Fortunately with the Internet, Skype and Facebook, I can still contact my family on a daily basis."*

Isolation

Is this enough? Whether it is or isn't, it is a fact that it is all we can do. I personally try to encourage my family to connect via Facebook and Skype as often as we can. It will strengthen the long-distance relationship between us all. There is a reason why long distance relationships are doomed, the simple fact that the people involved do not live close to each other. Because of the long-distance barrier, I have to work hard to ensure my children have a relationship with my side of the family. Being over here means I am cut off, out of the loop – it is my responsibility to keep in touch with everyone because they are all in one place and I am far away.

My son is very close to his British cousin who he sees regularly. And because they are growing up in the same country, their references, schooling and influences are the same. They have a lot to talk about (although ironically enough they tend to sit very close to each other NOT talking but madly playing on various console games) and enjoy spending time together. This is a lovely thing to witness and to nurture. So what do they have in common with their American cousins? Nothing. It is impossible to form this same type of relationship with them. I find myself forcing them to remember that they *have* American cousins. Perhaps when they are grown up they will have the opportunity to get to know their American cousins, their aunts and their uncles. Perhaps not. But what I can ensure is that his friendship with his English cousin continues and develops. Surrounding myself and my children with my husband's extended family is of great importance to me and means everything for my children. Essentially, their extended family is halved so maintaining a close relationship is vital. I am fortunate to have wonderful in-laws who we see regularly. Without them, I would truly be isolated and alone. Mollie comments on her in-laws:

> *"I have a very close relationship with my husband's family who are all supportive in many ways."*

I feel that my husband's family have accepted me as part of their own family as well.

Finding a support network through in-laws and friends helps tremendously but is not always possible. Not everyone gets along with their in-laws or has a close relationship with them. For some, raising their children so far away from their own families can be completely isolating. Melissa, American mum of two married to an English man shares her story:

> *"I found it incredibly hard to be so far away from my family. My mom would have been so involved with the children when they were young, and they didn't have that here. I always felt bad for them when I saw my friends' children and the relationships they had*

Isolation

with their grandparents. I know that my husband's mother loved them but she really only came to see them about three times a year even though we were only 10 minutes away. When I had my daughter, I decided not to go back to work full time, and although I really wanted to be home for the children, I was 32 years old and had always worked. So I found I really missed adult company. It was my friend who helped me the most, I had no support at all from family. I can remember telling my mother-in-law once that I was really homesick and she said it was my fault because I had decided to marry her son, so that is how much support I got. We did go back to the states at Christmas time quite regularly when the children were little, and they really used to love doing that. I think it was a combination of having family around and cousins their own age and different customs. I still miss my family, and I am really sorry that I cannot be closer to my sister. I also have missed seeing my nieces and nephew grow up. I just hope that when my kids have families my husband and I can reverse the trend and be a part of our grandchildren's lives. I am a strong believer in the importance of extended families."

Grazyna, a Polish mother of one with an English husband also comments:

Bringing Up BRITS

"My family members are really close so when I moved to the UK I felt very isolated. I didn't know so many things, my husband living so many years abroad, didn't know them either, my in-laws weren't aware of the cultural differences and I couldn't stand in the street and ask! Sometimes I felt like standing in the street and screaming! I went from a very busy work life and many friends to a monotonous life. Also, I am very conscious of my accent and feel that people don't want to talk to me when they hear my accented language. So it is even more difficult for me to make friends."

Grazyna touches on the difficulties of making friends which also resonates strongly with me as well as others. I think making friends is one of the most challenging aspects for non-British parents, in particular, mothers, living and raising their children here in Britain. It is also a vital lifeline and can act as a substitute for having our own families close by. To repeat what Nining said, her friends were her 'surrogate family'.

For me, finding friends and developing friendships has been an emotional roller coaster. When I first moved to England, the only person I knew was my husband – absolutely no one else. I actually suffered public humiliation over this when, in one of my Masters degree courses, the lecturer enthusiastically asked if I had told all

Isolation

my friends about my superb product design for an electric razor. I answered him by saying half sheepishly, half desperately, "I don't have any friends!" And although I was mortified, I felt a kind of relief in actually saying out loud that I didn't have any friends. It was my secret that was out so it didn't seem so bad any more. As I mentioned earlier, it wasn't until I had my children that I found and made good friends. Therefore, for me, I was truly dependent on my husband's family for support and friendship. Now, they are my 'surrogate' family here.

Thanksgiving is the time when I feel the most isolated from my family. Of course Thanksgiving isn't celebrated here at all and as it's arguably the biggest American holiday of the year, I miss it immensely. It's also my birthday and my dad's and my sister's birthdays all on the same day so my family's Thanksgiving celebrations were never a small affair. It's a sad time for me not being together with them. Skyping or talking on the phone is great, but it's not the same. For one thing, we can see each other but we can't hug each other. For another thing, it can be unreliable. The sound won't work, the video freezes, the children run off, the baby breaks the headset or worst of all, the Internet connection goes down. Then it's back to simply talking on the phone which just feels so long distance.

Bringing Up BRITS

Christmas isn't as bad because it's celebrated here, although I do miss my own family traditions. Consequently, I have instilled in my children, family traditions passed down from my parents. We do Christmas 'American' style in a sense because I ensure we do things like decorate the Christmas tree altogether as a family with festive music in the background and hot chocolate and marshmallows. We reminisce whilst picking out decorations saved from previous years and decorate the house with stockings and ornaments. I must admit, it is a real struggle to get my husband to participate as this is not something he is used to doing (and annoyingly doesn't take as seriously as I'd like him to). Perhaps one day my children will carry on with these traditions when they have their own families whether they are in Britain or elsewhere. It is my way of holding on to something precious to me, passing it down to my children and creating a secure, warm and loving environment so that being isolated from my own family isn't overpowering for me.

"The difference in parenting style and family values sometimes results in disagreements about how to discipline the children and what our roles as parents are."

This was another common response from parents when I asked them what was difficult and isolating about

Isolation

bringing up their children here in Britain, a foreign land. Being so far away from our own families and culture whilst raising our children is especially challenging when our family values don't comply with British family values and customs. One thing my husband and I argue about time and time again is the football. I don't want my son, or any of my children, to be exposed to football hooligans at such a young age and feel this type of environment is inappropriate for children. Nick totally disagrees and says it is a part of British culture and that all children – especially boys – should experience football matches. When I've mentioned this to other British people, they all have the same opinion as Nick.

Charlotte, a French mum says:

> *"There are disagreements over meal time customs. French meal time customs are different to British customs. All my family agree with me but my husband and his family do not think the same."*

Because we do not have our own families here for support and to strengthen our cultural influence on our children, it tends to be easier to conform to the British style of parenting, especially if our partners are British. Furthermore, if we haven't had the experience of raising children in our own countries, then it almost seems natural to follow the British model. However, if we come

Bringing Up BRITS

from a culture that is so very different with differing values and parenting styles, then it is challenging bringing up children in Britain as non-British parents. Estera, mother of one from Romania comments:

> *"The hardest thing for me about raising my child in a foreign country is the inflexible cruel go-to-bed-at-6.30-eat-whatever-you-give-them-must-sleep-through-shoudn't-pick-them-up-when-they-cry-must-do controlled crying type of parenting style 'forced' on one by health visitors, nursery nurses, other mothers, some of the English relatives. I bring up my child the way I feel and think best for her, and I wish no one interfered."*

Amy Chua, author of *Battle Hymn of the Tiger Mother*[4] describes the "Chinese Mother" and how she raised her children in America the same way in which her first generation Chinese parents raised her. She did not conform to the way Americans and the "Western Mother" raise their children but instead applied the strict Chinese model of parenting to raising her daughters. In her book she writes:

> *"Despite our squeamishness about cultural stereotypes, there are tons of studies out there showing marked and quantifiable differences between Chinese and Westerners when it comes to*

Isolation

parenting."

I think part of the way parents parent their children is because of the way they were, or the way they were not parented as children. However, there are additional cultural differences that can be challenging and isolating for parents who grew up in other countries and who are raising their British children here.

Linda, a Chinese mother of two says:

> *"I feel perhaps Chinese parenting is too harsh whereas I think British parenting is too lax – I feel I want to find the middle way. My husband encourages me and the kids to be more sporty and spend time in the country – he opens up a new world for me. He is influenced by me as well to push my children harder. We influence each other."*

Emilie, a French mother of one says:

> *"I think the parental model in France is [was?] more geared toward exercising discipline rather than being friends with your kids. People here are very "anti-smacked bottom" and reluctant to exercise authority. I am usually shocked at the attitude of kids toward their parents, in the way they talk (swear) and behave (hit). Our daughter is still small, but up to*

now, I have tried to be consistent and not to let her have any doubt that we are in charge and we know best. I do not aim to be my child's best friend. I'd rather be a good parent that sets boundaries."

I think lots of parents who are raising their children here, so far away from their own families find ways cope with feelings of isolation and loneliness whether through developing a close relationship with their in-laws or by surrounding themselves with friends who act as their 'family'. There are additional ways in which we are isolated – the difference in parenting style and family values plays a big role and one that is not always immediately obvious, but one that explains the emotions behind the experience. The physicality of raising our children in a foreign land impacts us greatly and often we are alone in that experience within our own family. That is an interesting place to be.

Chapter 3

Nurturing tradition: creating a multicultural family through food and meal times

Much of raising children revolves around food and supper time or as they say in England, "tea time". Childhood memories are full of meal times, foods we loved, foods we hated and traditions involving specific meals. For Christmas one year, my mother made a recipe book for me and my four siblings with recipes from our childhood. It includes foods she often cooked for us and still cooks at home, food we loved and associated with home and family. It is a much used resource for me and one that I too can add to and pass down to my children.

Ezra, one of Anne Tyler's characters in her acclaimed and popular novel *Dinner at The Homesick Restaurant*[5] is constantly trying to bring his family together and idealises the concept of family dinner through his restaurant. While he may not have been totally successful at this, what is apparent in Tyler's novel is that something as basic as food bringing family together, actually deepens relationships within a family which can, in turn, provide children with their own micro family culture within a culture. I certainly want to create and maintain a culture that encompasses both my American childhood experience with food and British meal time traditions. This may sound easy and one might wonder what the big fuss is all about, but when faced with cooking for a husband who expects certain English foods and shopping in grocery stores that do not offer those foods I grew up with, producing a consistent repertoire of American meals they will actually like and might even grow to love is no small feat. Perhaps I'm just culinarily challenged. But I haven't given up. I have found it takes a lot of persistence, nurturing and, failing inspiration, just plain old sugar and chocolate!

Foods I've introduced to our family that my children love: Mac and cheese for instance. Yes everyone can boil macaroni and make a delicious cheese sauce to pour over it and grill it in the oven. No, I'm talking about the original Kraft Macaroni & Cheese. The kind that comes in a box with a packet of powdered cheese that turns into a creamy sauce which is not only totally addictive but is part of every American's childhood memory. My husband pours scorn on it and my children love it. A fellow American mum of 4 shares my love and understanding of such foods. We exchange recipes and we are both known in certain circles for our American Brownies and Duncan Hines cake mixes. We get them from American Food

Nurturing Tradition

Director Skyco International foods, not all the time, just enough to satisfy our craving and create memories that our own children will have.

A few other foods I make are chocolate chip cookies, brownies, banana bread, PB&J sandwiches, tacos (becoming ever more popular thanks to 'Old El Paso') and chocolate fudge. Cooking, baking and eating American foods from my childhood is something my children and I can connect with, something they know is special and is American and therefore part of my background and their heritage. They feel they are sharing some little secret with me, that this is not something other mums make or do. Heidi, another American mother of 3, married to an English man says:

> *"Food is a big part of the way I introduce my American culture into my children's lives – making chocolate chip cookies! Peanut butter and Jelly sandwiches!"*

My children also understand the differences between American and English recipes in that they see me struggle with measurements. My American cookbooks call for cups and ounces or '1 stick of butter'. Butter does not come in sticks here but in large blocks! British recipes are all in grams and millilitres. I highly recommend investing in some kitchen scales; this has made my baking life so much easier! My son has a friend who absolutely loves my banana bread and I bake it especially for him when he comes to play.

Emilie, a French mum says that it is important for her daughter to experience her native food and traditional meals and cooks a lot of meat stews and vegetables. It is her hope that her daughter, who is half French half British, will learn these recipes too and will grow to love cooking traditional French meals. Julia, a German mum of one and one on the way also tries to expose her child to her native German food. She says:

> "I cook the occasional German-inspired meal, like Nurnberger sausages, Maultaschen, Kloesse etc. which I can partly buy at Lidl or Aldi, partly get sent from Germany by my family. My son loves the sausages but hasn't taken to Sauerkraut yet!"

Grazyna, a Polish mum, married to an English man, makes traditional polish goodies both savoury and sweet for her family. She too has an innate desire to instil in her daughter Polish tradition through food and recipes. Especially at Christmas, she makes a traditional dinner of carp with almonds and Kutia – a poppy seed soup which she and her daughter, Ania, make together and share with her English grandparents. Ania spoke of this meal:

Nurturing Tradition

"At first they thought it was strange but now they are used to it and realise it's important for my mum. And my dad loves Kutia. He can hardly stand up after eating it!"

Although they both mainly eat English food, these special occasions contribute to creating their own cultural family traditions incorporating both Polish and British food which ultimately helps Ania and her mum retain and nuture their Polish heritage.

There are other foods I have desperately tried to get my children to love such as ranch dressing, green bean casserole, sweet potato pie, pecan pie, and hash brown casserole without much success. I put this down to their age and try not to get too discouraged. There is still time and hope although, thinking about it now, I can't seem to get my husband interested in these either. I have not been successful in the slightest when it comes to Thanksgiving. Without there being an actual national holiday to provide enough time to create such a mammoth dinner or having access to such specific American ingredients, it is pretty impossible to replicate this American holiday and keep it going each year as a tradition. (You can get pumpkin pie filling from American Food Eat Direct though! See Resources) On the other hand, Larry, an American married to a British wife with whom he has two children who were born in England, has managed quite spectacularly to introduce and maintain such holiday tradition within his family. When my children were much younger, my family and I were fortunate enough to experience this feast and 'Thanksgiving' first hand. His children, now grown up and living in England still flock home for their annual piece of American pie.

Sari, a mum of 2 from Indonesia married to an English man, finds it so difficult introducing traditional food from her home country that she has mostly given up. She predominantly cooks British food.

"My husband prefers British food so I don't bother cooking Indian food. My children only eat British food."

Ahlam from the Emirates, mum of 3 married to an English man, also finds it difficult to cook food from her home country. Her husband also prefers British food as do her children.

"I'd like to cook more food from my own country and I do sometimes try. I make Salona Dejaj which is a chicken stew and my children love this dish. On the other hand, I want my children to fit in and be like their friends. They are growing up here in England so I want them to feel like this is their native country."

Nurturing Tradition

Ahlam makes a valid point and there is certainly some good advice in the saying *When in Rome, do as the Romans do*. Of course I want my children to feel at home in the country they are growing up in and even though I'm not British myself, my children are and therefore I want to help nurture that side of their culture as well as my own. And in practical terms, it's not all that easy to find the ingredients to actually cook authentic food from other countries. Lidl and Aldi are good shops to find European food ingredients. Specialty delis and foreign food markets offer opportunities for buying Chinese, Japanese, Middle Eastern and other Asian ingredients. Depending on where you live, it'll be easier or more difficult to access such specialty shops and food markets. (At the end of this book there are some useful websites for buying foreign foods.)

But these shops are not a one-stop-shop for all our grocery needs and can be more expensive. Plus, it is difficult to get away from the 'Made in Britain' and 'Love British Food' campaigns some of the major supermarkets and celebrity chefs continually champion. Sainsbury's, Tesco and Morrisons, Jamie Oliver and Gordon Ramsay all help to shape and influence what we cook, what our children want to eat and what ingredients are readily available. In families like mine, where one parent is British, we may accept this more easily and cooking typical British food might come more naturally. British food, traditional meals and eating customs may be a constant and effortless influence on our children. But what's it like for families where both parents are from foreign countries? Assia, a French Algerian mum of 3 whose husband grew up in Columbia says:

> *"I cook Mediterranean meals, French, Polish and now Colombian and British meals."*

Assia cooks traditional meals from her childhood such as couscous with chicken and black-eyed beans, meals based with lentils, white beans and other pulses. Their children love and enjoy this traditional food which, for them, is so much a part of their every-day life. Assia also tries to introduce British meals in order to provide a sense of ownership and belonging to the country they are raising their children in. Nining, an Indonesian mother of two half British children says she also tries to cook her native foods as well British food.

> *"I cook Indonesian food, at least twice a week. And they love it, even though I have to make it a little bit milder. Indonesian food is more like Chinese and Thai Food, with a lot of chilies, and spices. I have to reduce the heat so they can eat it without burning their mouth. But I also love British food.. I remember when I first came here, I couldn't eat British Food. But, now I cook British Food most of the time."*

Nurturing Tradition

Through food and meal times, Assia's and Nining's children are embracing British culture whilst associating their parents' native and traditional food with family, home and, essentially, part of their family's cultural identity.

In addition to the actual types of food we make for our children, meal time customs and traditions involving food also play a big part in how we raise our children. Fabio, an Italian father of three, living in England and married to a British wife, ensures his family all eat together as per the Italian model. If they lived in Italy where meal times are very family oriented, they would often include other extended family too. It's important to him to expose his British born children to this tradition from his own childhood and native country.

Eating together as a family is not emphasised in Britain as much as in other cultures. In addition, eating around the television is quite common here in England. It is also customary here for children to eat first (especially when children are very young) and then later on, the parents eat together without the children. Once, when a friend invited me and my toddler for 'tea' after our baby and toddler group one evening I assumed she meant for us all to eat together and so informed her that I was vegetarian (This of course was after I confirmed it indeed was for supper and not for a <u>cup of tea</u>!). This was a major faux

Bringing Up BRITS

,n my part which led to some embarrassment on part when she had to tell me she would only be cooking supper for the children. This was a brand new concept for me but one which I have accepted and implement during the week on a regular basis. At the weekends I do try to emulate my own parents' customs and create meal times where we all sit down as a family and share not only the food we're eating but each other's news and events.

One of my fondest memories from a very young age is of our family eating, talking and laughing together during supper time. When we visit my parents, this is a part of American culture that I know my children will experience. Charlotte, a French mum living in Glasgow says:

> *"French people are pretty obsessed with having dinner at the table together as a family. I tend to be very strict with that and my partner thinks I am too hard. But all my family and friends think like me – and all his family and friends think like him. Who is right?"*

I'm sure parents in general have their own ideas about food and meal time routines and the influence that has on their children, but when core values clash due to cultural differences, there is more to contend with surrounding those issues. It goes deeper than a simple

Nurturing Tradition

practicality of how and when to feed the children. It is about ideals, what we want to instil in our children, and how we want our cultures to co-exist and grow as a family. As Charlotte says, who is right? Finding that balance and getting it right, or simply not finding that balance and *doing what the Romans do* is an ongoing challenge and at times, a real difficulty and an uphill struggle.

In America, there is great emphasis on food as a form of social etiquette. When someone new moves into your neighbourhood, for example, it is customary for neighbours to make a pie or some cookies to welcome your new neighbour. When friends are sick or in the hospital, it is customary to make entire meals and bring them over or drop them off. Here, that can be misconstrued as nosey, interfering, and downright presumptuous.

Shortly after we bought our first house, my husband was so utterly horrified when I suggested taking over some cookies to our new neighbours that I've never mentioned doing any such similar gesture ever again. However, I often tell my children stories about when I was growing up, how we met and got to know our neighbours. My son, Samuel, totally loves the idea. He wants me to get to know the other mums at school and actually suggested baking cookies for them. Imagine showing up at the school gates handing out freshly baked cookies! Noriko, a Japanese mum of two, practically does just that – she runs a small business selling traditional Japanese sweets. After making them for the children at the Japanese club she helps run in Hove, the response was so overwhelmingly positive she decided to turn it into a business. Noriko now makes and sells 'Wagashi', sweets made with bean paste and sugar. Wagashi are traditionally eaten and given as gifts during Japanese celebrations.

> *"It is a bit like having hot cross buns for Easter or Christmas pudding at Christmas"*

In Japan, Wagashi is often presented as a gift when visiting family and friends and since presentation of food is an integral part of Japanese culture, the sweets are packaged extensively and beautifully.

> *"In Japan, the sweets are usually wrapped up in three layers, but I normally use just one layer of cellophane. The recent trend in packaging is 'simple is better' in the UK, and I try to follow it."*

Noriko successfully combines elements of both cultures, and in doing so, ensures her children, who were born in Britain, experience first-hand a custom and tradition of their mother's native country. Their Japanese heritage is

Nurturing Tradition

at the forefront of their upbringing. Noriko says:

> *"Wagashi is not only about food, it is about Japanese culture and art as well."*

The website for An-An is listed at the end of this book. Noriko's husband is Iranian and she feels it is important to include food from his culture as well. She makes both Iranian and Japanese meals which they eat together as a family.

> *"It can be make your own Sushi, Okonmiyaki on a hot plate, Sukiyaki hotpot, Tachin in a big pan or Kebab on the BBQ. My children now love eating most foods, and because of this, they do not have any hesitation eating traditional food when they visit their grandparents in Japan and Iran."*

Overall, exposing our children to our own cultural foods and customs whilst living in Britain, can sometimes be tricky and is often challenging.

One family tradition passed down to my husband from his family and one which is probably a tradition in many English households is Sunday roast dinner. It is greatly important to my husband that our children grow up with this tradition and look back on it with a feeling of warmth and nostalgia. Our children truly love this meal and love what it means to us as a multi-cultural family. For my husband and me it's about establishing a balance and exposing our children to both cultures. In our case, British culture will be the prevalent one but through food and traditional meals and meal times, we can create our own micro multi-cultural family traditions. And that is what it's all about really. That is what our children will take with them for themselves and maybe someday for their own families.

Funny story

The first week in our new life in Britain was just after Christmas 1999, we were living in Nottingham and I was a 'mature' student and Nick was unemployed. I came back from the grocery store with 6 boxes of mince pies. "They were only 30p!" I exclaimed excitedly, impressed by my ability to find a bargain and provide sustenance on a budget. Whilst I was beaming, my husband did not share my enthusiasm. He looked both sheepish and amused which I did not understand. "Mince pies are eaten at Christmas. No one buys them when it's not Christmas", he informed me. Oh dear. Nowadays, we always have a 'traditional' box of marked-down mince pies post-Christmas.

Chapter 4

Living and parenting amongst the British:
Are my children 100% British?

So far in this book, I've written about moving here and making a home here, isolation and the difficulty of raising children so far away from family, and nurturing traditions through food. What about living here, fitting in and adjusting to the British mentality and way of life? And what does this mean for our children?

My children never pass up the opportunity to point out my 'American' style of doing things in certain situations and I'm not sure if they view it as an endearing quality or if they are just plain old making fun of me! But what is interesting for me is that they tend to view it as *my* American 'quality' and not theirs. It's not something they necessary want to have ownership of but is fine for me to because I'm American. And although they recognise that they are half American, they don't actually see themselves as being American because of their British environment. When asked outright, they will unfailingly reply "I'm half English and I'm half American" because that's what they've been told and, for them, because they have both British and American passports, is a hard fact. It's more natural for them to feel British because, so far, that is all they know, this is their home, their birthplace and their first point of reference for absolutely everything. They only have me to influence them otherwise.

At school they hear their friends talk about American things and they tell me about American movies and they see various forms of American traditions on TV and read about them in books (and of course hear the majority from me) but they don't relate to American things as American children, they relate to them as British children. The world in which they are growing up in is totally different to the one in which I grew up. They see things through the British perspective, and although I consider this to be my home and can adapt somewhat to the British point of view, ultimately, my own children do not share my sense of what it is to be American and, no matter where they end up living, will always view the world through the British perspective.

On one level, I look at this as something that just is – we live here, they are growing up here so that is just a fact of life for us. And if it was the other way around and they were born in America and we lived there instead, my husband would be in my position. So, basically, it is what

Living and Parenting Amongst the British

it is. On another level though, I feel pangs of jealously that they have more in common with their father than with me. I have feelings of hurt and rejection simply because they are growing up British rather than American. But why? Why should it matter that they do not see themselves as being American and share my point of view? Why should it matter where they grow up? As long as they share my moral compass and view the world as I do as a fair and just human being, then what should it matter? Perhaps in the grand scheme of things it doesn't matter because I am a good mother and am bringing up my children to be good people. However, I think the way in which it does matter is because I inherently want to feel connected to them, to have a closeness with them, and sharing the same culture, cultural references and traditions is so much a part of that. It was slightly less imperative when they were babies because they didn't speak and there was a natural mother-baby bond that supersedes anything and everything else. Obviously there is still a mother-child bond, this will always exist, but I need to work harder at ensuring my children are American, and therefore like me, as well as British. I think this is why I force upon them certain American traditions so that they will experience American culture as first hand as possible and they will grow up with that as a point of reference. It will give them a sense of security and familiarity in their lives – they will be intrinsically British but also share American references. At least that is my hope.

Mollie, an American mother of 4 British born children, also sees her children as being British but tries to share with her children her own American traditions. She says:

> *"My children are British but understand alot of American words and phrases. I talk about calendar events that are happening in the States but don't always act them out. They understand the best that they can that they grew up and lived far away and that their (American) grandparents and relatives are not close by".*

She also comments on how challenging it is to maintain American traditions and celebrations. She says:

> *"It is always easier to have celebrations and events with more people and right now I don't have any other Americans to join in with. However, things like Halloween are becoming more popular and I put my own twist on events so they are more American".*

Molly's comment about it being easier to celebrate when there are more people to join in rings very true with me. Celebrations seem more significant when more people are involved and tend to be bigger and therefore more easily remembered. I don't have any American friends or

Living and Parenting Amongst the British

relatives nearby so everything that I do is for myself and my children only. It takes a great deal of effort and dedication to consistently celebrate traditions from our home countries here in Britain. Grazyna, a Polish mother of one, celebrates Christmas eve the Polish way despite having no Polish friends or relatives who live close by. She does this for herself but also to instil this tradition, the most important in Polish culture, in her daughter and make it an expected part of her British/Polish family customs. Grazyna feels that her daughter is more British than Polish. She explains:

> *"Although she was born in Poland, she is more British now than Polish. Yes, as much as possible. The hardest thing about bringing her up here is getting her to understand her Polish heritage, making her proud to be part Polish and not trying to hide it."*

I think it's a difficult thing trying to make children proud to be part American or Polish or Japanese or Swedish or whatever when they are growing up here. Ahlam, an Emirati mum of three, says:

> *"It's just me here so it's hard to show them how I grew up, there are no cultural references and nothing is consistent. They have their English culture which is where they belong – it's their culture and not mine."*

Bringing Up BRITS

Nining, an Indonesian mother of two says:

> *"By default, I consider my children to be British more than Indonesian because we live in England. They speak English, they eat British food most of the time, they are educated here, they absorb English culture."*

Julia, a German mum of one and one on the way says:

> *"My son is more British, as he lives here, all his friends are British, and he goes to nursery here. I try to speak German with him which was easier when he was home with me. Now he goes to nursery 4 days a week, he only seems to speak English, and I almost automatically speak English back. I hope with the new baby to be able to start again, speak German all the time, and keep it up with both."*

Linda, a Chinese mother of two British born children says:

> *"I do consider my children to be British. There is little Chinese influence because they go to school here and are brought up in English culture. However, I think my children consider themselves to also be Chinese – they are proud to be both and proud to be different (not sure how they will feel when they are teenagers!)"*

Living and Parenting Amongst the British

Heidi, an American mother of 3 is able to take her children back 'home', back to America, more often than I have. Her children have had more first-hand exposure to American culture than mine have. They can experience both cultures even though their predominant culture is British. Heidi says:

> *"My children like being a bit of both nationality. We have tried to make sure we get back to the States for some of the US specific holidays – even if it means taking them out of school. Halloween, and Thanksgiving in particular because they are both so unique to the US. It may also sound silly but the fact that they can watch the Disney channel in the UK meant that when we visited their cousins, and they were watching Zac and Cody or Hannah Montana, the kids loved the fact that they also knew about those shows and watched them at home."*

The simple fact that they can connect with their American relatives by identifying with the same television shows enables them to form a bond to their American heritage. Soila, a British/Kenyan mother who grew up in Kenya has two children born in Britain. She comments:

> *"They have both grown up knowing Kenya very well and speaking the language too (Swahili). I consider them to be mixed but they consider themselves more*

Bringing Up BRITS

British than any other nationality. Looking at my 19 year old, we have been going to Kenya every year since she was 18 months old. She knows her family there so well, she knows the country, she speaks the language and knows the do's and don't's of the culture. After her A levels she went and spent almost 2 months in Nairobi with my parents, siblings and their children. My 6 year old is very much looking forward to going back again this year. She understands the language totally and knows her family in Kenya too."

Not everyone is in a position to return home regularly or at all even, to expose their children to their own cultures so instilling in them a pride of their heritage or helping them identify with their foreign parent's culture can be a huge challenge.

I think one of the main factors for this is that our husbands, mine along with Heidi's, Ahlam's, Mollie's, Grazyna's, Linda's and Nining's are all British. Our children are growing up British with a British parent and in this environment we are the odd ones out, constantly trying to instil another culture into our family. It might seem easy to introduce non-British traditions and cultural celebrations, this is something all children experience, albeit perfunctorily, in British schools, but it's harder to *maintain* them and make sure they have meaning and

Living and Parenting Amongst the British

significance. Especially when our children experience them from one parent only – a parent who is trying to introduce something that doesn't fit in anywhere in the British calendar year or something that has a non-English name. There is no solidarity, we are on our own and although my husband will humour me by tolerating American traditions, it is merely a superficial acknowledgment because it is not his culture and we are not living in America. Assia, a French Algerian mother of three whose husband is Colombian has another view point. She says:

> "My children are European; I do not consider them to be British. Since they were little they are exposed to our different cultures, Colombian, French, and Algerian. At home I speak to them always in French and their dad in Spanish. We have friends from different nationalities and our children are exposed to those different languages, traditions and cultures."

Andreas, a Swedish father of 2 with a Swiss/British wife comments:

> "We find it helpful to read the ancient stories and myths from Scandinavia as they have a distinct cultural expression and also teach about the land. This has made my daughters understand that they have a rich cultural heritage behind them. Also we

celebrate the main festivals together such as Christmas and those from Scandinavia - keeping those main festival points alive with their songs and traditions also helps them gain insight to where they come from. Culturally speaking this is the hardest for a parent, as popular culture, has forgotten the older rooted festivals and myths or folktales which belong to a distinct culture."

Assia also brings to light another challenge for bringing up her children outside the cultures she and her husband grew up in.

"The hardest thing is the influence that other kids have on them and I try to remind them that we are not British and we have different rules."

Another mum, Claudia, and her husband are both from Germany and find it very easy to speak only German in their home and here in Britain. It is their first language and although their children speak English at school, when they are at home they are able to seamlessly switch over. For Assia, Claudia and those families where neither parent is British or grew up in Britain, there is a mostly non-British influence in the home. Perhaps this makes it easier to instil pride and understanding of their heritage in their children.

Living and Parenting Amongst the British

To answer the question posed in this chapter's title, "Are my children 100% British?" - no I don't think so, and not just because they have American passports in addition to their British ones. I believe that my own cultural influence makes them American as well. Even though they are growing up in Britain as British children, they are also a part of me and I am not British.

Interesting quote from my husband Nick BEFORE he read this book:

> *"Our children are totally assimilated into British culture. They are 100% British and in no way at all American. In a way, they view you (Meghan) as being British in that they make no allowances for your being American."*

Soila's story

"My eldest daughter and I were just about to land in Nairobi. It was early morning and we had a window seat. I looked over and I said to her, "Aaah, finally we're home." She replied, "Your home mummy, not mine." How true I thought. How true. She holds a French passport and was born in Britain to a French and Camroonian Dad and Kenyan Mother. She is not confused, she knows where her home is and I am glad."

Living and Parenting Amongst the British

Nining, from Indonesia, with her British husband and their children

Grazyna, from Poland, with her British husband and their daughter, Ania

Bringing Up BRITS

Mi, from Sweden, with her son

Mollie, from the USA, with her British husband and their children

Living and Parenting Amongst the British

Assia, from Algeria, with her husband, from Columbia, and their children

Heidi, from the USA, with her British husband and their children

Bringing Up BRITS

Noriko, from Japan, with her children

Arianna, from Canada, with her daughter

Living and Parenting Amongst the British

Estera, with her British husband, and their daughter

Meghan, from the USA, with her British husband, Nick and their children, Samuel, Anna Grace and Jonah

Photo by Mi Bewick Photography

Chapter 5

Cross Cultural Kids, Third Culture Parents

Regardless of where we are from, we share the commonality and emotional journey of bringing up our children in a culture that is not ours. David Pollock and Ruth Van Reken[6] describe children who are raised outside their parent's home cultures as *Third Culture Kids*.

> *"A Third Culture Kid (TCK) is a person who has spent a significant part of his or her developmental years outside the parents' culture. The TCK frequently builds relationships to all of the cultures, while not having full ownership in any. Although elements from each culture may be assimilated into the TCK's life experience, the sense of belonging is in relationship to others of a similar background."*

My children are not Third Culture Kids in that their father is British and they are being brought up in Britain, their father's culture. So, they may indeed have full ownership of being British and naturally assimilate to Britain. So how

Cross Cultural Kids, Third Culture Parents

much of an influence do we non-British parents have on our children? I definitely feel like a *Third Culture Parent*! According to Ruth Van Reken, it is clear that my children are indeed *Cross Cultural Kids*.

> *"A cross-cultural kid (CCK) is a person who is living or has lived in –or meaningfully interacted with-two or more cultural environments for a significant period of time during childhood (up to the age 18).*
>
> *We define these particular groups of CCKs in the following way:*
> *Traditional TCKs: Children who move into another culture with parents due to a parent's career choice.*
>
> *Children from bi/multicultural homes: Children born to parents from at least two cultures. May or may not be of the same race."*

Although they are growing up in one of their parent's home cultures, they are not growing up in both their parent's home cultures simply because those countries are different. Assia and Claudia's children, on the other hand are closer to being TCKs although some of their children were born in Britain. Heidi's children are experiencing life in China, having been born and lived in Britain with an American mother. They are TCKs and CCKs. I see in my children my American qualities and although right now, as mentioned in chapter 4, they view them as being my American qualities, it is something instilled in them from a young age. They are growing up within a bi-cultural home.

So, as parents bringing up cross-cultural children, we share an experience, regardless of specific details. Some of the cultures we come from may be extremely different to Britain, others more similar. On the surface of it, it may seem no different to living and raising a young family in the United States – the language is the same, both countries celebrate Christmas and are allies politically, and both countries have freedom of press and speech. But, unlike Britain and EU countries, my husband and I cannot live in both places together without visas. I think bringing up children in a foreign environment, even if you've not had the experience of bringing up children in your native country, is challenging on a practical level and also on an emotional level. Eileen, a British mother of 3 spent nearly 10 years in Holland before having children. When her first child was 18 months old, she and her Australian husband decided to move back to Britain to raise her family. Eileen says:

> *"And so it came that we moved back to the UK when Kyla was 18 months old to give her that traditional British upbringing and schooling that I felt had served me so well".*

Cross Cultural Kids, Third Culture Parents

For Eileen, there were some aspects of Dutch culture that she did not want instilled in her children – she wanted them to grow up British and in a country she herself understood and whose values she shared. Emotionally, it can be a wrench knowing that my children are growing up predominately British and not immersed in American culture and in the 'world' I grew up in. Perhaps other expat parents feel the same about their home countries and their children. I think we cope with these emotions in our own personal ways. One reason I wanted to write this book was to simply say to all expat parents raising their children in Britain, "Hey, you are not alone out there!" I also wanted to illustrate some of the practical challenges we, as third culture parents, come across on a day to day basis.

For me, the school system is totally different, I find the medical terminology to be outrageously different, and social etiquette and customs mystifying and difficult to get to grips with. I once made the colossal mistake of providing my child's party guests with party favours instead of party bags, therefore disappointing everyone and stigmatising my child! Perhaps on the one hand these are superficial challenges that are overcome in time. However, I'm not sure the learning curve ever becomes less steep. This may be true for any new parent British or non-British. But I do find I am disadvantaged, often confused and have to ask questions I feel I should already know the answer to. I didn't understand what a registrar was when I was in the hospital. I spent one of the most vulnerable and painful times in my life wondering why the person who was supposed to be in charge of record keeping was considered to be the most senior medical person in the room. And why are doctors addressed as 'Mister' Instead of 'Doctor'? Also, I had no idea that you couldn't take your child to the doctor for a check-up unless something was actually wrong with them and even then doctors seem to think it's not entirely necessary. I had to ask my eldest son's teacher to show me how they teach basic addition and subtraction – exactly how it's written out on paper. I felt like an idiot! But I simply had to ask in order to help my son with his homework as I was showing him the way I learned in America which was completely different, therefore confusing him even more. I had to learn the British way in order to help him. Arianna, a Canadian mother says:

> "I'm very nervous about my daughter starting school and worry that I won't be able to help her with her school work or help her to learn".

Nining, an Indonesian mother of two, comments:

> "If I have questions about the school system, I just log on to the computer and do some research. Thanks to the Internet, there are a lot of websites that can help

Cross Cultural Kids, Third Culture Parents

you understand the education system in UK."

Although it isn't too difficult to find the answers, it does take more work and I am forever in doubt. Besides, the Internet doesn't cover everything about British culture and some ways of doing things don't come naturally to me. At times I find myself lacking confidence where I normally would not. There are so many things we need to know but we don't actually *know* that we need to know them until we are smack dab in the middle of a situation. Furthermore, there are aspects of British systems we disagree with. Arianna says:

"I don't know anything about the British education system, but what I've seen and heard of it I'm not that keen on it. I don't agree with uniforms. A child is an individual and should be seen as one (within reason of course), and I don't find that the classrooms here have very much space at all."

Emilie, a French mum married to a British husband, is also apprehensive about her daughter going to school in Britain. She says

"I am very unhappy about the curriculum here, the schooling mentality, the educational values. The curriculum allows too many gaps and prevents children to achieve their potential."

Bringing Up BRITS

She believes core skills like numeracy and literacy are not mastered by the time children go to University. For Emilie, the French educational system is preferable over the British educational system. But she is living here with her British husband, raising her half British daughter who will be immersed in a completely different schooling ethos. Heidi had the experience of having her children in the British state school curriculum but now is dealing with an International school curriculum in China. She explains:

"I do feel that in the UK system you may need to make a bit of a fuss to get the most out of a school. I can only say this now as I look back and see the difference in math level that my daughter is experiencing at her new school in Beijing. She was in the middle level at her old school in the UK and I have recently said to my husband that it appears that unless you are in the top level you are kind of forgotten about. I think that the UK system is not great for the good kid who is studious, pays attention, doesn't make any trouble but is middle of the road in the core subjects – I just think they get left to their own devices because they don't cause any trouble. Whereas if your child is very bright and top of their class in various subjects they seem to get every opportunity to shine that comes along. I feel that my children are getting more of a chance to

Cross Cultural Kids, Third Culture Parents

shine where they are now and it has really highlighted the issue in the UK for me."

I sometimes worry about guiding my children through their educational journey. I can't understand the way the school system works for teenagers here. Why should 16 year olds have to apply to go to high school? It seems to be a very negative and challenging process. Doesn't this create an unnecessary and complex barrier that can actually discourage kids to go to school? I talk more about this subject in chapter 8, so will briefly say, I am panicky about getting to this stage with my children and resent the fact that mandatory school stops at age sixteen.

In addition to the practical challenges of living and raising my children here in Britain, a culture different to my own, I find it emotionally challenging because of a need to assimilate into British culture, make friends and have a strong sense of belonging here. Whilst my children are growing up here and going to school here, I want to fit into their world. So how do we fit into their world? Estera, married to an English man, feels Britain is her home and the transition from living in Romania to living here, for her, was made easy because of her husband and daughter who was born here in Britain.

Bringing Up BRITS

"This is home for her. I feel I belong here as well. My family is here, my daughter and husband – I belong wherever they are."

I think belonging here is something that non-British parents of British children struggle with in different ways. Sometimes some sense of belonging is found through their children, their British husbands, through work or friends, and in many other ways, a sense of fully belonging remains elusive. Emilie describes her feelings about belonging:

"I kind of belong here, but I'll never belong anywhere, I've moved too much. My daughter probably does belong here, although I'd rather she didn't.

And to repeat what Grazyna says about belonging:

"I still haven't found my place here."

For me, I still struggle with elements of belonging here. In most ways I feel this is my home, my children were born here, I have a successful career here, and I am creating a future for my children here. But I don't belong here the same way that my children and husband do. Firstly, I don't have any history here in the same way that my husband does. He has his school friends here who have known him for years, and there are so many different parts of his life that are all referenced here, and of course he has his family here. So this is his home, his world and he belongs here in that sense. For me, for one thing, I don't necessarily see us living here indefinitely – we might make a home for ourselves in America perhaps, so in that sense I am only living here temporarily which makes belonging here a totally different thing for me. My husband and children will always be from Britain and they will always belong here even if they move away at some point. They will always belong here whereas I don't in that same sense. I am also very aware of my 'foreignness' here, I am reminded of this literally every day by both my husband and my children!

Although I am immersed in British culture, I have no ownership of it – I'm an onlooker, observing and gleaning what I can in order to belong here, to fit in and make friends. I think making friends here and fitting in is done very differently to the way it's done in America and perhaps in other countries too. It's more subtle, takes a long long time and the rules are incredibly vague. When I first moved here, I was at a total loss in social situations. I felt completely inept at conversing, ill equipped because I didn't understand the jokes and references that people were talking and laughing about (for example, references from British childhood television programs, TV and radio presenters, British mainstream culture, British pop stars etc.) and constantly had the distinct feeling I was being made fun of (I'm sure I was, but it was so indirect that I couldn't defend myself or else I would look like a complete weirdo). I literally didn't know what people were talking about because I didn't grow up in Britain so felt unable to join in and therefore not really a part of the conversation because I didn't understand the jokes or references and couldn't add in my own because nobody would know them. Nobody ever tried to explain anything either, so basically I felt hideously uncomfortable and like a complete jack ass. And although it gets easier the longer I live here, I'm still baffled by the British sense of humour and the banter style of conversing and am still occasionally offended.

I'm also often gullible, whereas before moving here I wouldn't have said I was a gullible person at all. It's not exactly clear cut if people are joking or being serious and it's difficult to work out what exactly is being said or if anything is being said at all in fact. I find this to be true in both social and work situations. I think the way things are phrased, sometimes very indirectly, makes it difficult to know how to respond or gauge what the situation is. I think this makes British people seem more stand-offish and therefore forming and maintaining friendships is tricky and at times, hard work. I don't think British people are stand-offish necessarily, they just appear to be because of the type of language that is used, especially when you first meet them. I don't want to be overly stereotypical because there are always exceptions and I have met British people who do not seem stand offish from the onset. However, I do find it to be a completely different ball game when it comes to getting to know people and making friends. Heidi comments:

"I would sometimes get frustrated by the fact that British people just never seemed to be that interested in getting to know you unless there was a specific connection already established. This would apply to conversations with strangers at a party my husband and I may have attended. You would start a conversation and I remember often commenting that it seemed very hard to keep it going in that the other person would rarely ask me a question to keep things going. I also noticed that in America you would keep a conversation going just to be polite, even if you didn't agree, or weren't interested. However in the UK I found that people would just stop a conversation dead in its track with a strong disagreement or dismissal of a topic."

I can definitely relate to what Heidi says! It all contributes to the emotional difficulty of being so far from friends and family in the States. Noriko, Japanese mum of two says:

Bringing Up BRITS

"Some people, especially parents of children's classmates, are not very friendly at the beginning. In English social life, sharing humour is thought to be very important. So once they realise we know quite a bit of English jokes, they start to open up. It takes time though."

Tiffiney, an Australian mum of one reflects:

"I miss the friendliness of Australians – this was the case before I had my son as well."

Nining, a Muslim mum of 2 from Indonesia comments:

"I try my best to be friendly with everybody, but again sometime it seems like a wall is dividing us. Being a muslim – with hijab/ scarf — can be tricky as well, can make other parents reluctant to approach us. But I never make it a problem."

Linda, a Chinese mother of two British born children talks about the way she's adapted to British culture in terms of how she relates and interacts with people. She says:

"I have adapted to my husband's way, the British way but I want to be more open towards other people. British people are more private whereas in china we open up more and we experience each

> *other's problems together more. I think the Chinese way is better and I hope I can improve on that – I feel I have adapted to the British way on this and I want to bring back my Chinese influences."*

Making friends with British people takes time and patience and a lot of the 'getting to know you' stage. Adapting and fitting in also means we might need to change the way we interact with people, change our own expectations and just go with the way things are here. This in itself can take a while to actually recognise and come to terms with. It can contribute greatly to feelings of isolation, loneliness and frustration of not being in our 'home' countries with our own families and friends close by.

Growing up in America, there was always encouragement to look on the positive side and to be optimistic and *carpe diem* – seize the day. It was the norm to have high expectations of things and of people. I've always had a *CAN DO* type of attitude and been surrounded by people with the same positive outlook on life and situations. I feel it is very different here and that filters down into the way things are done, like meeting people and making friends, like schooling and opportunities for young adults. Mollie, American mother of four comments:

Bringing Up BRITS

"I find mainstream British people very negative and accepting of mediocrity. I also don't think Brits value education as much. When I was at school it was assumed I would go to college [uni] I have the same expectations for my children. "

I want my children to grow up feeling that they can achieve anything they set out to achieve. That although life is full of challenges, they will be able to overcome them and be successful in their lives by using the tools they are taught whilst they are young. And one of those tools is having a positive outlook on life and using that outlook to be proactive in both their personal and professional lives. I try to be a positive and inspirational role model for them as a working mother and to lead by example. Running my own business entails a plethora of skills, requires high motivation and the ability to carry on through hardship, stress, disappointment, difficulty, and situations beyond my control. And although I don't share every detail with my children, I inspire them to be the same in both work and in general. I think there is a common complacency amongst the British. That life is viewed as such a struggle, that there are stumbling blocks which, no matter what, cannot be overcome. It's all doom and gloom. People grumble about things, but then don't actually do anything to change the situation. There is an unspoken etiquette: don't rock the boat, don't say anything that might cause offence. Emilie comments:

Cross Cultural Kids, Third Culture Parents

"I hate the 'sitting on the fence' mentality"

People would rather suffer in silence than dare to say anything that might embarrass or offend someone else. Obviously I'm not saying every single British person is like this nor am I saying all non-British people are not like this. In part, this is an endearing quality of the British – the mindset of 'have a cup of tea and it will all be fine' type of mentality. Without actually doing anything to make it fine. However, for me, this is a major cultural difference, one that is prevalent in the way I raise my children whilst living and working within British culture. It's not something which comes easily to me so I cannot understand it from the British point of view, and it's also something that I don't want my children to encompass.

I think I have influenced my British husband! He used to complain to me about bad service or a faulty product but then wouldn't take any action to rectify the situation. Instead of complaining alongside him, I would say, "So, do something about it. Call them back / tell them they made a mistake / tell them you are unhappy with the service"...or whatever the situation was. Nowadays he automatically takes action; sometimes he skips the complaining stage and cuts straight to the action. Unfortunately, this doesn't exactly apply to when he's sick or in pain – no matter what, he refuses to go to the doctor or take pain medication. This may be just a 'man' thing though rather than a cultural difference!

I think he also values the importance of openly celebrating achievements and occasions (something Americans are very good at doing and yours truly is no exception) which is something he wasn't used to doing before. It's important for me to outwardly encourage and celebrate what my children do. I don't think it comes completely natural for British people to openly recognise and celebrate things in the same way. It is more understated and unspoken but not necessarily less significant. It is a cultural trait that is hard-wired into us.

On the other hand, I have found my perspective has changed because I live here and I have definitely somewhat assimilated into the British way of life. In a way, it is imperative for me because of my children who are half British and who are growing up here. I think it's natural to want to fit in and to do so almost seamlessly.

Here are some comments from my contributors about how they have adjusted to the British mentality and assimilated into British culture:

> *"I don't feel so foreign anymore. I speak the language (better than most Brits!!!) and feel very integrated into this life." – Mollie*

Cross Cultural Kids, Third Culture Parents

"I queue, I am less confrontational. I love tea." –
Emilie

"I have adjusted to the British mentality by children
having their tea early, not calling people for business
purposes during the weekend, not going to visit
British people without arranging a time, not
commenting on negative things I have noticed about
the person or someone else." – Assia

"More realistic portion sizes! The sense of excess is
ridiculous in the US however I do remember very
clearly asking Pizza Hut delivery when I first relocated
from the US if this was seriously their largest pizza!!!!
It seemed so small and there was no extra large
option – I am embarrassed I did that now but that
always reminds me of how my mentality has
changed." – Heidi

"I've learned to love the countryside, sports and
gardening" – Linda

"I have been here 16 years so I almost feel like a
local! I have adjusted to being inside so much more,
I've gotten used to this – no choice really! I have
also gotten used to there being so many more people
around in small spaces. I found that really hard in the
beginning." – Tiffiney

Bringing Up BRITS

"I think there are things/rituals that we do differently and I have adjusted to those in terms of need. For example, we, as Kenyans tend to go and see a person at home without the need for an invite and we won't feel like we are imposing but that we are looking after. Here people don't do that because it's considered to be imposing so I have adjusted to this." - Soila

For some cross-cultural families living and raising their children here in Britain, the challenge is not just trying to assimilate into British culture it's being able to raise their children outside of their native countries, but within their own religion. Nining, a Muslim from Indonesia is married to an English man who is also Muslim. They are raising their British born children in England as Muslims. Nining explains the challenges:

"My husband and I try our best to raise our children as good Muslims, as we both are practicing Muslims. We put Islam/Muslim as our first identity before anything else. We have taught the girls about Islam since they were young. They are involved in every religious ritual and they go to the mosque to learn about Islam and Al Qur'an. I think raising Muslim children in this country is the hardest thing because some western values/cultures are not parallel with Islamic values. Some of them are even

against Islamic values. But we don't want our children to be a fanatical, short minded muslim. We want them to understand and apply Islamic values in their daily live, but we want them to respect other values as well. So that's maybe the toughest challenge for us as a parent to raise our children here in this country. If we bring up the girls in Indonesia, where the majority of the population is Muslim, we wouldn't have this problem as we share the same values."

So to conclude this chapter, as "Third Culture Parents", we may deal with getting to grips with British systems, social etiquette and living amongst the British in different ways, but we share the commonality of raising our children in a foreign environment. Even if you've not had the experience of bringing up children in your native country, there is an even higher and more complex learning curve. It is challenging on both practical and emotional levels because we are not British, we did not grow up here yet we must assimilate into British culture as our children are naturally immersed in it. We are ultimately all raising cross cultural kids (CCKs).

"While the idea of CCKs is a growing concept, there is one thing we know for sure that virtually all CCKs share: by definition, each of them grows up in some sort of cross-cultural lifestyle or environment, no

matter the particular circumstance." - Ruth E. Van Reken[6]

So as parents of CCKs, we share challenges and the emotional journey of raising our children in Britain, outside our own native countries and cultures.

Chapter 6

Lost in Translation: Language barriers and miscommunication

The first time I ever got confused by a British expression that meant something totally different in American English was in an expat bar in Prague, overcrowded with Brits way back in 1994. (Incidentally, this was the same night I met my British husband.) One of my fellow teachers at the University also taught at the London School, a British language school, and had invited us out with her British co-workers. Part way through the night she came up to me, put her arm around my shoulders and exclaimed, "I'm pissed!" To which I replied with great concern, "Oh no, what happened?" She just laughed and stumbled away in to the crowd, leaving me baffled. It wasn't until later that I learned that 'being pissed' in British English means drunk. For me, the only definition of 'pissed' meant to be really angry at someone or something. So there marked the beginning of a lifetime of confusion for me.

Bringing Up BRITS

Actually, when I moved to Britain, I didn't think language would be an issue at all. Why would it, I thought. My first language is English so it seemed like it would be an easy transition – no new language to learn. In reality, there was indeed a whole new language to learn! British English! Plus, there were all the regional expressions and terms of endearment to become familiar with. One day in a shop in Nottingham, an elderly man called me "Duck". Duck??? That was an odd one. But he was so kind and sweet that I couldn't be offended! The British lexicon opened up a whole new world to me and was a constant reminder that "I'm not in Kansas anymore!" There are some words and expressions that I have fallen in love with and some that I absolutely despise. One expression I just hate is 'get on'. To get on with someone or something. It just sounds wrong to me and in American English it means to actually get on someone else – like actually get it on with someone in a romantic way! Perhaps the British English word I find the silliest is slippy. "Be careful, the floor is slippy." Ugh, sounds like a made up word or a word you would only use to speak to a small child which you shorten to make it easier for them to say. On the other hand, I probably overuse the word lovely. It's just such a lovely word and one that Americans don't often use, or at all in fact! I also love the expression 'to pop by'. "I'll pop by around 4pm" – it's just such a scrumptious thing to say!

Lost in Translation

There seem to be quite a lot of Americanisms that are becoming part of the British lexicon. In my opinion, most don't really work purely because they are pronounced with a British accent. A classic example is "that sucks". This is a quintessential American expression that I often hear British people saying. It just doesn't sound right! I find it comical and slightly annoying. I suppose it's like Americans trying to say 'bollocks'. We put the stress on the wrong syllable making it sound like a completely different word. That might seem comical and slightly annoying to British people. Anyway, it seems the American lexicon is crossing the pond, thanks to E4 and Sky, and becoming all too familiar amongst the British. The next generation won't even be aware that they are Americanisms at all. Of course I do not mean to suggest that British people sound American or constantly use American words and expressions. On the contrary, I am always struggling to choose the right phrase or words in any given conversation. I am often openly mocked and made fun of (mostly in jest I'm sure) because of the way I speak. At times I do not fully understand the gist of a conversation because of the subtlety of the British language and somewhat evasive way of conversing. The longer I live here, the better equipped I become. However, my accent is a constant reminder to me and to those who know me that I am not British. It is a part of me that I cherish and would hate to lose altogether. The danger of losing it is only too real. Friends and family in

Bringing Up BRITS

the States tell me I sound English because of the way I speak – the stress I put on syllables, the way I accentuate a phrase, and the words I choose simply because that's what everyone here says. For example, I now say 'property' instead of 'real estate'. 'petrol' instead of 'gas'. 'motorway' instead of 'highway'. 'nappies' instead of 'diapers', 'chips' instead of fries'. The list goes on! There is a chance that when my children are grown up, I will sound more like them than like my own parents. However, I think my accent is so much a part of me and is part of my history and heritage that I don't want to lose it. It's a paradox really. I'm desperate to fit in here for myself and for my children, but I don't want to actually *sound* British. One thing that will always give me away as being American is my unfailing use of the word 'bathroom' instead of 'toilet'.

Before my children went to school, they had a distinctly American twang to their accent and even pronounced some words in American English. I was thrilled! Only to discover that it completely disappeared the moment they started school. They constantly correct my pronunciation and even mock my accent and poke fun when they are annoyed at me. (Especially if I am scolding them or issuing instructions – and actually my husband is the worst when it comes to poking fun at my accent). There are times when I don't even understand what they are saying and vice versa! I think our communication is very

Lost in Translation

cross-cultural. One of my oldest son's favourite words is 'awesome'. I use this word quite a lot too but it sounds totally different when he says it.

They are always asking me what the equivalent word is in American English. And they consciously choose to use the British word. For example, they prefer Father Christmas to Santa, shop to store, mummy to mommy, toilet to bathroom, sledging to sledding. They sound British so I tend to think of them as being more British than American. Yet they are my children and I am American. There are some exceptions to this which I find very interesting. They say dessert instead of pudding, peanut butter and jelly instead of jam, and supper or dinner instead of tea. They also pronounce yogurt the same way I do with long 'o' instead of 'ya' and put the stress on the first syllable. It's probably the ONLY word they pronounce the same as I. I wonder what it is about these words in particular that they use them as Americans in an American manner. And why is it only those few words? When I asked them about this they answered:
Samuel:

"Mummy, I only pronounce yogurt the American way at home. When I'm with my friends I say yogurt the normal way."

Bringing Up BRITS

So I guess I was deluding myself a tinsy tiny bit. Clever boy.

Anna Grace:

> *"I say yogurt instead of yogurt because I'm half American".*

Duuh. She also said:

> *"I don't know why I say jelly — sometimes I get confused and say jelly at school and my friends ask me if jelly is jam and I say yes".*

Giggle.

Mollie, another American mother with 4 British born children is in a similar situation with her children. She says:

> *"I do speak American for a lot of things and teach them both words. They don't have my accent."*

I also teach my children both words, but it is a challenge because my husband usually butts in and tells them to use the British word. He'll add in a quip about sounding like a loud American or something which although mildly amusing, isn't very helpful to me! Arianna, a Canadian

Lost in Translation

mother of a British born daughter comments:

> *"I say words a certain way and I am forever being corrected by my British in-laws. I don't want my daughter to have to be corrected as she is both Canadian and British and therefore both ways are correct."*

Although both ways may be correct, the British way is the 'normal' way of pronouncing words here and using certain British words is a constant element in my life. I tailor my vocabulary to fit in with my British family, my children pronounce words in a certain way to fit in and be accepted by their peers. It's a natural way of adapting to an environment and finding acceptance. It's challenging culturally because it's adopting another form of language, of learning new words, new expressions and new ways of communicating.

What about actually having to learn a new language all together? Not just different words and word usage in the English language. For those parents whose first language is not English and who are raising their children here in Britain, language must be a massive challenge. Some parents might be able to speak English, some not very well and some not at all. But it is essential for their children to speak English. Certainly young children will find it easier to pick up the language because of school and since they are young, it will come naturally to them. However, there will inevitably be difficulties for parents raising their children bilingually. Emilie, a French mother of one says:

> *"I sometimes try to bring my child up bilingually, but not strictly. I speak French to my daughter seldomly. I struggle to switch back to French."*

Aja, a British Slovakian mother of two who is raising her children bilingually says:

> *"I do find it difficult as on many occasions I just forget to speak to them in Slovak and find it easier to talk to them in English."*

Linda, a Chinese mother of 2 is raising her children bilingually. She comments on the challenges and says:

> *"It's challenging because of the lack of language environment in general. I think there is a Chinese school that would be good to send my son to. I don't know of any parent support groups."*

Andreas, a Swedish father of 2 daughters says:

> *"The most important factor has been to try and teach our daughters Swedish and also French, this has been*

Lost in Translation

*a challenge – having a teacher "outside" of the family
has helped a lot with this."*

Soila, a British mum who grew up in Kenya is raising both
her children trilingually. Her husband is Danish and the
father of her first child is French and grew up in
Cameroon. Her cross-cultural children are immersed in 3
different cultures and 3 different languages. Soila says:

*"My younger daughter seemed to have speech
problems (which she has now overcome) and she
understands more than she speaks Swahili and
Danish but that will change I am told. Her English,
both written and spoken is very good."*

Since I personally don't have this clearly challenging
experience, I would like to share the stories of two
parents raising their children multi-lingually.

Firstly, Noriko, a Japanese mother of two British born
children, ages 7 and 4, is married to her husband from
Iran. They are raising their children in a trilingual
environment, teaching them to speak Japanese, English
and Farsi. Noriko speaks to her children in Japanese but
the primary language in their home is English and her
childrens' primary language overall is English. English is
also their preferred language. Noriko comments:

Bringing Up BRITS

"I sometimes find speaking in English easier, however, I do try to speak Japanese to the children at all times."

For Noriko, it is important to her for her children to be able to speak her native language. Although English is the predominant language and essential for her children to speak, she says:

"Language is a part of my culture that I need to pass on to my children. It's the same with food and annual occasions. There are so many customs we cannot communicate in English. Only in my native language can I explain so many things about Japanese culture. It's also important for opening up their future on an international scale. I believe they will come across new languages in the future."

Teaching and encouraging her children to speak Japanese in their British home is challenging and inevitably difficult. Noriko explains:

"They understand and speak Japanese, however, if they need to explain something complicated, they prefer speaking in English."

Noriko's children attend Japanese school, a school which Noriko set up herself, every Saturday morning. She says:

Lost in Translation

"There is a large Japanese community in Brighton & Hove and I started out by setting up and running a toddler group for Japanese families to play in Japanese."

This outlet is a lifeline for her and for other Japanese/British families. It's immensely important to find support and other families in similar situations. It helps Noriko's children to bond with their Japanese culture and learn their mother's native language. Unfortunately, some parents are not so lucky to have a community of their own nationality or schools and toddler groups in their native languages. Estera, a Romanian mother of one, married to a British husband, said this was a difficulty. She explains:

"Romanian being a small language is not taught anywhere here in Britain and there are no playgroups for Romanian speaking children".

So Estera is bringing up her child bilingually in an isolated environment, unlike Noriko.

Raising her children in a multi-lingual environment is definitely a trial and error learning curve for Noriko and her husband. She said the first step was the most challenging for them and for her son.

Bringing Up BRITS

"Even at two and a half years old, my son did not speak a word. He was in a very confusing world – English from nursery, Japanese from his mum and Farsi from his dad. We thought we needed to take him to a speech therapist. Once I gave up the trilingual environment, he immediately started to speak English, in perfect sentences even. 4 years later we started to teach him Japanese and Farsi again. It might be much harder but now he understands why he has to learn them and he speaks in the other two languages very well."

When asked about her children's schools and if they were supportive or not, Noriko replied:

"Their school is aware of them studying other languages other than English. I indicate this during the first consultation every year. Most teachers say as long as the child is not behind the other students in English, they can prioritise Japanese and Farsi homework."

It must be extremely challenging for them and for Noriko to make sure they study all three languages. It's triple the work-load of regular students! Noriko says that is precisely one of the negatives of raising her children trilingually – she has to force them to study languages twice or three times more than their classmates. When asked about the positives, she said her children speak in Japanese and Farsi to their extended families. She also says:

> *"My son is now very proud of being Japanese-Iranian English."*

Noriko is trying to give her children the best start in life growing up in Britain and being part Japanese and part Iranian. She ends by stating:

> *"I am still ahead of my children in terms of knowledge of English. One day, it will be turned around...."*

Grazyna is a Polish mother whose daughter, Ania (Anna in English), was born in Poland. In 2003, when Ania was five, Grazyna moved them to Nottingham, England to be with her British husband and they have been living in Britain ever since. Grazyna says:

> *"She became fluent in both Polish and English from age 2 and 3. Then her first language was Polish and now her first language is English. I communicate with her half in Polish and half in English. When she has friends over I speak to her in English only. I make an effort with this because I don't think it's nice to speak in a language together that her friends won't*

understand. They might think we are saying something bad about them. I often mix the languages – there are some words in Polish that don't exist in English. When we are in Poland visiting my mother, we only speak in Polish and she can switch to fluent Polish there."

Ania comments on speaking Polish:

"When I'm in Poland, I immediately speak in Polish. My first language was Polish, but I'm much better at speaking English than Polish. Here, I have a Polish friend at school and although we mainly speak English to each other, we do sometimes speak Polish together. I prefer to speak English because it's easier. I sometimes mix the languages and if my brain is not working properly, sometimes a word comes out in Polish when I'm speaking English and vice versa."

Grazyna feels that it is important for Ania to be able to speak Polish for two main reasons. Firstly, it is part of her Polish heritage and being able to speak the language means she can feel a part of what it means to be Polish. Also, when she goes back to Poland, she can feel more at home, less like a foreigner and therefore feel 100% part of her Polish family. Secondly, being bilingual could open doors for her when she is at University and beyond – generally, it opens up more opportunities for her.

Lost in Translation

Grazyna says:

> *"I think that my family would feel really hurt if they couldn't communicate with her. Because she lived in Poland for 5 years, it's really important for her to know the culture and to keep her heritage. And for the future, the opportunities she will have by being bilingual. Especially now, the world is more accessible and you never know where you will end up working and living. She's richer because she knows and is immersed in another culture by speaking Polish. I also think being bilingual makes it easier for her to learn another foreign language, like Spanish for example. She will have advantages when she is older."*

One of the main challenges of raising Ania bilingually for Grazyna is finding the time to converse only in Polish together. When Ania was younger, this was not such an issue because she was the main carer for her and she wasn't independent. It's also difficult to find places where they can go to speak Polish. Although they go to Polish church where there is a small community of Polish people and they can speak Polish together, there is not a big Polish community where they live in Worthing. So there's no real outlet for them to go and speak only Polish. Grazyna says:

"With her being older now and being more independent, I don't find so much time with her on my own when we can speak Polish together. I cannot make her speak in Polish to her Polish friends or with others There is no support network for us. When we were in Nottingham, there was a Polish school that she went to. But here, it's a small place for one thing, and also I don't know as many Polish people here. There is a big Polish community in East Midlands and there isn't anything here. There's no demand for it as there are so few Polish children here. So that is difficult for me."

Another challenge is making sure people outside the family are aware that she is bilingual. Her schools do not automatically assume she is bilingual because her name doesn't sound foreign. Grazya explains:

"She's not treated any differently at school because teachers don't realise that she is bilingual. I have to make them aware of the fact that she's half Polish and she speaks Polish. It is strange because she has an English surname and a first name that also sounds English so no one knows that she's bilingual or that she's half Polish. I had to let the schools know that she is bilingual. Although I put on her form that she's bilingual and needs to have the Polish GCSE, they didn't read it properly because I suppose they didn't

Lost in Translation

think they needed to so they didn't enrol her in Polish
GCSE and I had to point that out to them."

Because Grazyna is fluent in English, she doesn't find speaking English a difficulty, but what she does find challenging is other people's perception of her English ability because she speaks English with an accent.

"I have felt discrimination in a subtle way. I have to be twice as good as British people because of my accent. At school, some students don't trust my knowledge of English. They don't believe that you can have a perfect understanding of the language if your pronunciation is different. I find that hard because I know my knowledge of the language is very good and my level of English, both written and spoken is very high. With Ania, my awareness of the language (the structure and grammar) is higher than hers but Ania's English is more natural and she doesn't have my accent."

When asked what she thought was the biggest challenge for Ania, from Ania's point of view regarding her bilingualism, Grazyna replies:

"I don't think she's ashamed of speaking another language but I think for her she feels that she is a bit different from other children. It's not a bad thing, it's

good, but I think sometimes for her, she knows that she's a bit different. It helps her but it is also difficult for her. Her father actively encourages her to speak Polish. He's very happy that she speaks Polish and wants her to continue as much as possible. He is very supportive of bringing her up bilingually"

For Noriko and Grazyna, despite the challenges, raising their children bilingually and trilingually in Britain has many benefits. Noriko and Grazyna are providing their children with a strong link to their own cultures through their native languages.

In a way, although American English isn't strictly a different language, I am also instilling in my children the sense that they are American as well as British by maintaining my culture through language, the American vernacular and lexicon.

Lost in Translation

Funny story

It was Christmas time when I first moved here and my future sister-in-law kindly invited us to spend New Year's Eve with them. She said the whole village parades around from pub to pub in fancy dress and it's "loads" of fun. I immediately started to panic. "I don't have anything to wear!" I exclaimed. She said not to worry, that something would sort itself out. Well, I didn't know what that meant and to me fancy dress was a ball gown and black tie affair. I was stressed for days wondering how on earth something was going to sort itself out. This was, after all, my first social engagement in this new country in my new life in England, with people I didn't know and I didn't want to stick out like a sore thumb or make a fool of myself. On the night I didn't want to go but couldn't do anything about it and when I mentioned to my husband that we were supposed to be in fancy dress, he just laughed and said it was OK, that it wouldn't matter too much. I nearly cried. When we got there, to my utter relief and ultimate surprise, we were presented with blonde wigs and ridiculously long fake eyelashes! Well I didn't make a fool of myself, but I certainly felt foolish! If only I had had a dictionary of British English words (see Resources). A translation: Fancy Dress in British English means to dress up in costumes. In American English it would be called a costume party.

Chapter 7

Celebrating Britain: What we are giving our children

There are many positive aspects about bringing up my children here in Britain, a country in which I myself did not grow up. I think there are fantastic benefits too, and so far my experience has been interesting, educational and generally very good. Of course there are drawbacks and hardships as well – a lot of which I have explored in previous chapters, but I want to concentrate on the positives whilst writing this chapter.

One of the best things for me and my children is the fact that we are close to mainland Europe. In the US, travelling from State to State could take 8 or 10 hours (and even much longer!) – but if you travel 8 to 10 hours here, you could be in France or Germany or even Italy! It's fabulous. My kids are already so knowledgeable about European countries and cultures. When I was their age, I didn't have first-hand experience of any countries outside America, apart from Canada and Mexico. And Canada didn't really feel like a different country at all! My

Celebrating Britain

children are growing up with a broader world view, which will no doubt be an important benefit for them when they are older. Even at the young age of 6, my daughter understood concepts about travel, nationality, language and culture that I wasn't introduced to simply because of our geographical placement. Both my older children are learning Spanish, French and Italian at school – not formal language classes, but they are learning expressions and songs and they are very aware that people come from countries other than Britain. The fact that these countries are close by, means that Europe as both a concept and as a physical place can be attainable and accessible – a reality. For me, Europe was an abstract concept and it wasn't until I was at University that I actually travelled to any European countries. At that point, my whole life view encompassed so much more, I felt more knowledgeable about the world, current affairs, and basically just felt smarter. This is happening to my children now, at a young age, and I think it's absolutely wonderful. They certainly wouldn't have this to such a high degree if they were growing up in America simply because of the sheer vastness of America itself. There is a physical (and financial) obstacle, so travelling to Europe for a long weekend isn't something the average American person does but *is* something the average British person does. My English nephew went to Paris on a school trip – for me, this is fantastic. The opportunities for European travel that my children will have, and already have, will give them the best start in life and opportunities that I did not have when I was their age.

Another great thing about raising my kids here is that they are effortlessly exposed to so much history and great architecture. Castles, cathedrals, abbeys and historical country halls and houses can be part of a normal weekend day out. For me, I am constantly amazed at what we can see and learn about first hand and have hands-on experience with. And even everyday things, like cobbled streets, Victorian terraces, Edwardian tiles, thatched roofs, dry stone walls, and tiny lanes are a constant affirmation that history is piled upon history and we live in and amongst antiquity. I am giving my children the opportunity to live and grow up amongst all this. I realise that this is normal for them – they probably even take it for granted. However, the mere fact that we can have lunch in a seemingly ordinary pub and there will be a significant history about the place. I think growing up with that is wonderful. It's not just Europe either that they are immediately exposed to. There are more international influences that we are exposed to whilst in Britain. Because America is such a large country, by default the majority influence is American. But here, the rest of the world seems so much more accessible. Heidi, American mum of three half British children comments:

Celebrating Britain

"I prefer the British news and feel that we get a much more balanced, global view of events than you do when you watch US network news. I do remember thinking that it would be hard to go back to such a US centric view of the world after having my eyes opened by my time in the UK."

Another truly wonderful thing about bringing my children up here is the fact that we can walk so many places. It is the norm to walk to school as opposed to going in the car. Here, we are not completely reliant on a car and, in general, there is more of a walking culture here. Unless you live in the inner city of a major US city, you must have a car, so you must be able to drive. Americans have been known to jump in their car to collect their mail from the mailbox at the end of their driveways! It is certainly not the case here for the average resident. Being able to walk everywhere encourages and influences my children to rely on their own ability to walk in order to get from A to B. Even when we lived in Nottingham, a much bigger place than Worthing, we were still able to walk to school, to the local shops, and to the park. I think there is such a huge emphasis on being able to drive in America. Children start learning to drive at age 15 and are legally able to drive at 16 once they pass their driving test. Here in Britain, although children are able to take a driver's test and get their licence, it's not such an essential part of their childhood. It's not as common or popular. I was learning to drive at the age of 15 and by the time I turned 16, I was driving every day to school, to work and goodness knows where else during the weekends. The thought of my own children driving at the tender age of 15 makes me want to break their legs! Luckily, this won't be an option for them. They will learn to drive when they are older, and even then, won't have to depend on a car to the degree that I did. Heidi comments:

> *"I also loved being able to walk places and not being stared at because unless you live in a city in the US it is rare to walk anywhere!"*

The simple fact that things are physically closer here in Britain makes walking and walking culture a part of the way of life. In addition, we are never completely isolated from civilisation – this can be important whilst having young children. Even when we were on a remote farm in Wales, we were still only a 15 minute drive to a major grocery store, cafes and shops. Tiffiney, from Australia, comments:

> *"Australia is a wonderful country but unless you live in the city it can be quite isolating in itself as most Universities and work opportunities are in the cities. My son will live a life in the "country" here in Britain but be very close to Brighton and London. You wouldn't get this in Australia without having to drive*

large distances."

For many parents, another positive aspect about raising our children here in Britain is the fact that there is so much encouragement in schools. Teachers and educators openly encourage children, there are opportunities for them to develop, express themselves and learn the skills they want and that will set them up for life. For me, I do believe they would also have these same opportunities if they were growing up in America. However, some of the parents I interviewed feel very differently. Assia, who is French and grew up in Algeria states:

> *"I think my children are very lucky. I would have been very sad if they were in Algerian school where we were punished physically and where our self-esteem was very low. Children are more confident, can give their views, and are respected for that. Children are given the opportunities to participate in afterschool activities, have all different trips with their school, do different activities during school hours, and are more aware of what is going on in the community. In my case, the school was only an academic place where we went and sat for hours to learn."*

Grazyna, mum of one whose daughter was born in Poland but is growing up here says:

Bringing Up BRITS

"I feel very happy about my daughter attending British school. It gives her much more opportunities to develop her interests and talents. Children don't feel so much pressure every day, they are not tested so often."

Nining from Indonesia, mum of two half British children comments:

"The government really put the young generation as their priority. In Indonesia, education and health services are very expensive. Not just that, but the quality of education and health service in England is far better than in Indonesia. In some ways, bringing up children here is safer as well. And as a parent, I just want my children to be healthy, safe, happy and have a good proper education. They have a good education here."

I think it is clear that educating our children here in Britain is definitely a huge positive and although experiences will vary, it is certain that we are giving our children the best possible start in life.

The NHS is another benefit to some foreign parents raising their children here in Britain. It's free! Ok I know it's not "free" and we pay for the NHS and medicines in taxes, but there are no huge medical bills, I didn't have to take out a loan to give birth to my children and paying in taxes makes it more manageable financially as opposed to paying for each separate medical requirement or emergency because you don't even notice. I didn't have to go into debt or pay off hospital bills when my children were born, and there was no pressure or worry about medical bills each time I gave birth. I know the cost of the medical bills weighs heavily on some people's minds when they really should only have to think about giving birth! It can be a huge stress that people having children here don't have at all. Heidi says:

"I think that the NHS is an amazing system for the most part!!!!! I had all 3 kids at an NHS hospital and my sisters could not believe that we had health visitors come to the house after the children were born. Despite their expensive private insurance they never had anyone visit the house. I also think the mid wives are doing an amazing job. To think that people in the UK can lose their jobs and not worry about medical care for themselves or their families is a huge benefit that is not enjoyed by people in the US. People in the UK take the system for granted and I think that the NHS should start sending out bills that are representative of the cost that would have been incurred if they had to pay for the treatment themselves – people would quickly realize the benefit of this system."

Bringing Up BRITS

Nining says:

> *"I have to admit that NHS is brilliant. If you come from a country where healthcare is very expensive, having a free treatment is amazing. I had two caesareans when my girls were born. In Indonesia you have to pay lots of money for the operation. But here everything is free. I have a very friendly GP who is really helpful whenever we need his help. I know that sometime you have to wait a long time before you have your medical treatment. But, hey... it is still better than many other countries...So be grateful for it."*

Mi, from Sweden, says:

> *"I think the NHS is great and I can't imagine any worse system than in, for example, the USA. No-one should ever need to feel they're being hindered from receiving medical treatment if they need it."*

Soila from Kenya comments:

> *"My experience with the NHS has been nothing but positive. People say that I am lucky but I have not had any negative experiences. Not for me or my girls. I think it's terribly great that it exists, that's for sure."*

Celebrating Britain

I also think it's amazing that children under 16 can have free prescription medicine. It may seem trivial, but it actually eliminates any financial stress whilst having a sick child. This can make a huge difference to your everyday lives.

Depending on where we come from, we will all have different points of views and might have different positives and reasons for what we think is great about bringing our children up in Britain and why. However, the rewards of bringing our children up in Britain are many and range from simple things like experiencing Autumn and snow to more important issues like having a good education, freedom of speech, human rights and an affordable health system. We are giving our children a good start in life and, as parents coming from other countries and cultures, there is much to celebrate about Britain. Britain gives our children a positive future and many great and wonderful opportunities.

To conclude this chapter, here are some comments from some of the parents who contributed to this book.

> "I love that my son experiences traditions and seasons here. You don't get these in Oz." – Tiffiney

> "I think our children have a lot more opportunities than us. They live in a free and stable country where

they can develop, where they are guided in every step they are taking in life at home and in the community." – Assia

"Culturally, it is a bit challenging because I have to balance Indonesian culture and British culture. In my opinion, bringing up my children in this country makes them more aware with the diversity of its people. Hopefully makes them more rounded as a person, and more tolerant to other differences". – Nining

"People here are very child-friendly." – Claudia

"I'm pretty sure the maternity and paternity pay/leave is much better over here than in Canada (I think we get a longer maternity period here). The 15 free hours of nursery sessions is again something that is offered here but not in Canada." – Arianna

"They are very close to their grandparents in the UK as we have been able to spend most Christmases and Easters with them. I also loved the fact that I never had to drive in the UK – we used public transport extensively due to our proximity to London. I also like the fact that the UK does seem less pressurized in terms of consumerism. In the US you just tend to buy more stuff just for the sake of it. I also like the fact

that the kids grow up walking everywhere. We also travelled Europe extensively so that they have experienced other cultures from an early age. The proximity of so many amazing museums, galleries, history etc was something that we really do take advantage of – and we never had to get in a car!" – Heidi

"I believe my children have any opportunity to be successful if they are willing to work hard. They have the best of both worlds. They have a good education here, and they also have Eastern/Islamic moral values from my country." – Nining

"My children have a lot more opportunities to learn different things apart from academic studies. Like swimming lessons, sports and after school clubs that are non-academic. My childhood was more focussed on academic studies so i am happy to be able to provide various educational things for them." – Linda

"I love London. I love the life in terms of ease of moving around, the night life, the British sense of humour, the politeness that allows me to get on with what I need to do without feeling attacked or picked on for being different." – Soila

Chapter 8

The Future: It's really just the beginning!

Well, this is pretty much the end of this book. However, I think it's just the beginning of my life as a foreign, expat parent to British children. Whilst my children are young, they are naturally assimilated here, feel at home and feel British. What about when they are older? As they grow and develop intellectually, will they develop a different or altered cultural identity because their mother is from a different country and is of a different nationality to them? I suppose a lot of that depends on how much or how little I actually influence them. Perhaps if we are able to travel back to the US more often, that would make a difference. Perhaps at some point in their lives, they will spend a significant amount of time there which will in turn strengthen their American roots. I see in my children my American qualities and perhaps this will strengthen the older they get. Perhaps they will reach a time in their lives when they question their cultural identity.

The Future

My own mother is originally Canadian but eventually became an American citizen. She is married to an American and had all her five children (two are adopted from Korea) in America. She also had a career in America and still lives there today as an American citizen. So, she is pretty much all-American now. For me, as a child, although I didn't feel Canadian or have Canadian citizenship, I did feel an affinity to Canada on one level. I had Canadian grandparents, a Canadian Aunt and Uncle and cousins the same age as me. We visited them often when I was young and I spent many summer vacations at a summer camp in Ontario. I understood it was where my mother was from, all her family still lived there and it was a different country. As a place, it only felt vaguely different to the US but it never felt like home. I suppose although I viewed my mother as being Canadian, I also viewed her as being American and especially so once she became a US citizen. This was probably mostly because there's not as much difference between the two countries as compared to the difference between, say, Japan and Britain where the cultural differences are great. So, despite my efforts to make my children feel American as well as British, will they feel *only* British when they are older? I can't recall my mother ever foisting upon us Canadian culture, however, by spending a lot of time there and having a relationship to her Canadian family, our own family felt closely linked to Canada. As an adult though, I never felt Canadian nor ever considered moving there or spending time there as opposed to living in the US. My sister, on the other hand, says:

> *"I do feel an affinity for Canada. I have very fond memories of time spent there. Both in Toronto and up at camp (mostly the time outdoors). I am not a Canadian citizen nor do I have dual citizenship. Mom is a US citizen now. I have thought about going to live in Canada, from time to time, and think it would not be difficult for me to get Canadian citizenship, because of mom and our family connections."*

So perhaps, like my sister and me, my own children will feel differently to each other about their being both British and American. One major difference is that they do all have dual citizenship and will be able to live in one country or the other when they are adults.

One aspect of my children's cultural heritage is their racial make-up. They are half Korean by race. Whilst they are young, this is something that has not been an issue for them and we as a family have only briefly talked about. Once I was chatting with a furniture store owner who 'complimented' me by saying "your English is really good". I replied, "Thanks very much!" Having experienced these types of comments all my life, I am used to them and understand that because I look Korean, people might

The Future

think I actually am Korean. So their perception of me is totally different to who I actually am and what my own perception of myself is. That is, and has been part of my everyday life. When people first meet me, they ask me where I'm from and when I answer that I'm from the US, they look quizzically at me and I feel obliged to then add on that I was born in Korea. The relief on their faces is priceless! They then think they understand that I am actually Korean. So I then have to explain that I was adopted by American parents and was raised in America.

Something I find fascinating about my own racial identity is that I don't feel Korean and never did feel Korean when I was a child. And, interestingly, I have more memories of my mother foisting Korean culture upon me as opposed to Canadian. She wanted me to feel proud to be Korean and not marginalized at all because of it. In her mind, she had adopted me from a country with a rich culture, was bringing me up in America as an American child and wanted me to have an affinity with Korea, which was my original ethnic background. She bought me Korean dresses and dolls, books with Korean babies and children in them, books about adoption, she made kimchi and other Korean foods and she talked a lot about my Korean heritage. At the time, as a child who just wanted to be the same as everyone else, I rejected all this – I didn't want the fact that I looked different to be pointed out in obvious ways. I felt embarrassed about being different and ironically, this was exactly what my mother was trying to guard me against. However, as an adult, I understand and can appreciate what my mother did for me. There was never any question that I was adopted and came from Korea, where people looked different to Americans. And even though I don't have an affinity to Korea and Korean culture (probably mainly because I grew up in America), I do understand my mother wanting to keep my Korean heritage alive for me.

With my own children, I am keen for them to feel American but I don't necessarily care if they feel Korean or not because I never did. When my mother came to stay with us here, she brought Korean baby dolls as gifts for my children. So, again, she is recognising their Korean background when, in fact, I don't. For me, this is a very personal challenge and one that is quite difficult to articulate. My oldest child once told me someone called him Chinese. He didn't understand this and just shrugged his shoulders. I told him it's because I'm Korean so he's part Korean. He just said 'OK'. I think the difficulty is that I feel 100% American but I look 100% Korean. I have an American upbringing and background, not a Korean one. And because of this and the fact that I rejected everything to do with Korea when I was a child growing up in America, I don't see it to be a necessary part of my own children's upbringing.

The Future

My husband, on the other hand, thinks it may be important to talk about this with them so that as they grow up, there is no question about their racial ethnicity. So in addition to instilling in them a sense of their American heritage, perhaps I also need to instil in them their Korean heritage as well. I think if I was actually from Korea, it would be natural for me to expose them to Korean culture. However, because I am not Korean, in the sense that Korea isn't my culture, it means that I see them as being British and half American with Korean nowhere in the mix. Despite this, because of how they look, perhaps I need to view them as being 100% British, 50% American and 10% Korean so that they will too?

Because of their young age, they don't think they are anything but British (and part American) and feel just like their class mates and friends. But what about when they are older and they become more aware of their racial differences to their British peers? It's a real challenge for me because I don't have any inclination to flag up the fact that I'm Korean but for the sake of my children and their own cultural and racial identities, this could be important for them.

I am also concerned about potential racism towards them because they are not obviously British and they are half Korean by race. They look different and in my experience, racism is horrible and comes in all different forms, from outright verbal abuse to seemingly innocent but ignorant remarks and assumptions. My oldest child has already experienced racism to a certain extent in school with another child assuming he was Chinese. And although that child probably didn't think he was saying anything wrong by telling my son he was Chinese, the mere fact that my son was called Chinese brings the issue of him being Korean to the forefront for me. Because of his age, he didn't understand why he was being called Chinese but I can guess it made him feel a bit strange and view the experience as being negative. Luckily, the schools are very open to discussing these issues and are very pro-active when it comes to teaching about different races, so that is positive. But it won't necessarily prevent any racial comments or behaviour towards my children. I think because of my own experience, I want to protect them from this and don't want them to feel that they are any different racially. I think the challenge for me is that I want them to feel proud of what and who they are as individuals, which would encompass all elements – British, American, Korean – but since I don't necessarily have any connection to my own Korean heritage, how can I instil that in them?

Interestingly, when I asked the contributors if they had experienced any kind of racism and if they saw this as being a potential problem, most of the responses were no. Perhaps this is because people in general are less

The Future

racist nowadays maybe due to more awareness in schools and in the media?

Assia comments:

> "We have never experienced any sort of racism here. People are very tolerant and very respectable."

Soila, a British/Kenyan mother of two says:

> "I lived in France for 2.5 years and I experienced more racism there in that short time than I have in the 20 years I have been here in Britain – overt racism or otherwise."

Mi, a Swedish mother comments:

> "I have only experienced racism towards other people, and it´s shocking. Mainly from older people. As I´m white and my English is ok, people (read taxi drivers) can start talking about immigrants in a negative way with me. I usually reply "immigrants like me you mean?" which makes them very embarrassed."

Nining says:

Bringing Up BRITS

"So far I don't have a physical racism attack. Some of my friends who wear hijab have had some kind of racism attack, being called names, being spat at, or had very impolite remarks especially from the youth. I hope my children will not face any problem being a mixed race. I think British people are getting used to mixed races. What we can do is to teach our girls to be kind, polite, and be proud of the way they are."

Nining can celebrate her Indonesian culture and race and instil in her children pride and a connection to their race. For me, I find it easy to instil in my children pride that they are American, but it is much harder to help them feel proud of their Korean race when I did not grow up in Korea and rejected any Korean influence because I wanted to be the American girl I viewed myself as being.

Looking a bit more into the future, a few practical things I am concerned about as a non-British parent raising teenagers here is the whole schooling system for older children and the pub/binge drinking culture that is the norm for British teens. Firstly, the school system – I don't understand why 16 year olds have to apply to go to high school. If they don't get into the school of their choice it might discourage them to actually go. And the fact that mandatory schooling ends at age 16 means that they can actually stop going because it actually physically ends. In the US, legally, teenagers can drop out of high school at

The Future

the age of 16, however since high school is 4 years and finishes when teenagers are 18, they just continue on seamlessly. There is no definitive break when children are 16 – school doesn't finish until all four years have been completed. I never even considered not finishing high school when I was 16. It does make me worry that I will have to convince my children to go to high school when I feel that is something they should do automatically and without question. My other concern is that they will have to choose their specialized subject so early on. Teenagers here must limit their studies to a few disciplines rather than study a broad range of subjects. Why must they do this so young and so early on in their studies? What if they don't know what they want to be or what they want to study when they go to University? Yet they have to choose what they want to specialise in which therefore determines what they study in high school and at University before they even get there. Arianna says:

> *"I do have concerns with regards to parenting my child in Britain when they are in their teenage years. It's mainly the school system as it's very foreign to me and I don't understand all of this stuff about GCSE's and A Levels and that."*

I don't understand any of this either so will have to learn it before my children reach this stage. I do find it difficult though, when I disagree with the system in general.

Bringing Up BRITS

Grazyna is raising her Polish born pre-teen daughter here. Grazyna is also a teacher in a British high school. She comments:

> "I am aware that British education is not as good as in Poland. Basic subjects like English and Mathematics are lower and schools in general are not as strict. It's difficult because I know she would get a better education in Poland, but I wouldn't want to move her away and make her go to another school as it would be very difficult for her – a big change as they are stricter and tougher there. It's very tolerant and supportive here. But that is also a problem. The kids don't realise how easy they have it here. In Poland, you have a lot of homework and more tests/exams. They have a shorter amount of time to learn things – they just have to learn it."

Heidi comments:

> "I think there is something great about the collegiate atmosphere of US high schools and Colleges. However I always liked the thought of the kids growing up in the UK, near London where they could get around on public transport as young teens. I knew then that their US cousins would love to come over and experience that side of our culture."

The Future

I suppose the real challenge for us will be what our children, as teenagers, do that will be so different to what we did as teenagers. I think parents in general worry about parenting their teenagers, but for me and other parents like me, who did not grow up here, there is an element of the unknown and an element of what we imagine might happen it to be by observing what we see British teenagers doing. Linda, a Chinese mother of two says:

> *"Teenagers here are more materialistic because of the society as a whole is more materialistic. There is less respect to teachers and elderly. Society is more individualistic so people think about other people less than in Chinese society."*

My husband imagines that our sons will like going to the football, going to gigs and hanging out with friends drinking beer in pubs because that is what he did as a teenager. For him, there is no question about it and sees these activities to be the norm for teenagers in Britain. Whereas I had a completely different experience as a teenager in that I had my own car, I drove myself around to school, to friends and to my part-time jobs at the weekends. We never hung out in bars or pubs because we couldn't, but also because most of the socialising was done at the actual high schools themselves – football games, pepper alleys, dances and socials. This brings me to my second main concern about parenting my British children when they are teenagers. Even though, by law, teens are not allowed in pubs until they are 18, they tend to go when they are 16 or 17. It's totally normal for teenagers to drink in pubs. I balk at the thought of my children going to pubs when they are 16. For me, it is a totally foreign concept. Pub culture is very British and something I did not grow up with whereas my husband did. So although he is not thrilled by the idea that our children might be going to pubs when they are 16 and 17, it is not something he cannot fathom. Does this mean that there are fewer opportunities here for teenagers? What are the alternatives? In the States, the norm is to work part time after school and at the weekends. Nearly all of my friends in high school had jobs. It was part of our 'coming of age' in that we earned our own money, learned new skills(s), took on the responsibility of having a job, learned through experience the value of money and began to form a work ethic. I think it will be very different here for my children in that they won't want to get jobs because their friends aren't doing that or because there are few opportunities to get a job as a 16 and 17 year old.

Julia, a German mum, expresses her concern:

> *"I am worried about how bad teenagers' reputation is here. I am concerned this will make them feel*

The Future

useless and unappreciated, and lessen their chances of making their way. They don't deserve to be seen as waste of space or even threats (in general opinion and media), before they even had the chance to prove themselves."

Emilie, a French mum says:

"My daughter is still small but my main concerns have to do with the provision of education which I find sub-standard in terms of breadth and depth compared to "Continental" education, the lack of mentoring and positive role models, and the poor attitude in term of hard graft and achievement."

So perhaps we, as non-British parents to future British teenagers need to work harder to ensure our children have the experiences and opportunities we desire for them. From my point of view, coming from perhaps the materialistic capital of the world, I find consumerism and materialistic attitudes to be far less than in the States and feel that is a positive aspect to bringing up my children here. But I can relate to what Emilie says about lack of positive role models, poor attitudes towards hard graft and achievement. I feel I will need to push my children and help them to broaden the boundaries and look beyond what is immediately on offer for them. Perhaps many British parents feel this way too, but I am approaching this from a different point of view with a different cultural reference and therefore feel that what the norm is here, should not be what my children should strive for.

Looking further into the future for my children growing up here, I am afraid for them financially. The cost of living is so high here, many young adults are staying at home for longer as they are not able to actually afford to move out, let alone buy a house. I don't want my children living with me when they are in their 20s, they should be out there doing their own thing and living their own lives, but they might not have the liberty to do so because it's simply unaffordable. Do I pack them off to the States? Should I be prepared for them to live at home much longer than they should?

And finally, there is the dilemma of what I do when my children are grown up. Do I stay here or do I convince my husband to move to the US so I can finally go back home? For me, the chance to live in America and go home again has great appeal for various reasons, but I am afraid that if my children remain here, then I will miss out on their lives as adults.

Mollie comments:

"The only dilemma I have with having a family in a

The Future

foreign land is what I will do when my children grow up. I would like to return home eventually and it will be very difficult if my four boys are scattered around the UK and US. Either I go home without them – but what for?! Or I stay here with them and their families and never have the chance to go home. Sigh. I hope I will have the financial liberty to travel more when I am older."

Emilie says:

"I do not see myself retiring in the UK, and in my mind, there is always the possibility that we will one day return to France."

Heidi comments:

"Until this most recent move to Beijing I always saw us staying in the UK although I thought that the children would travel and would probably live elsewhere and we would visit them wherever they were. I definitely thought that our proximity to Europe and the fact that the kids were exposed to different cultures, at such an early age, would mean they were more open to living abroad. Now I am not so sure where we will end up in the long run as it is still early days with this relocation. Things like the short vacation days in the US always stopped me

from wanting to return there permanently as it makes work/life balance much harder than it already is. So that is definitely something that the UK has going for it!"

Julia says:

"I can't see myself moving back to Germany when my children are grown up, as I now feel quite rooted here. I will, however, support my children if they wish to go and study or work in Germany, and might even go back to live there for a while. I might want to be closer to my family when my parents get older, but in general this will feel like a step backwards. I have been there and done that, and I have moved on! A totally new country seems more attractive as an option."

Although, like Julia, I do feel rooted here for many reasons, mainly because of my family and my career, there is always an inclination to one day go home. I do get excited whilst thinking about returning home and living in America again. However, will I feel like a foreigner in my own country after having lived and worked and raised a family outside of my home country for the better part of my life? How difficult might that be and would it be worth it? Each time I go back and visit my family in the States, I inevitably fantasize about moving

The Future

back, about the type of house we could buy, the land we could own and the lifestyle we could have. But furthermore, what would that mean for my husband when all his family are here. One major concern I have is when my parents are older and I am over here. How will I help take care of them? Will I need to travel back and forth more to help them? If so, how viable financially will this be in that will I actually be able to do that? I would like to be close to my parents in their old age, but with my life and my family here, that poses a huge dilemma and causes me great concern.

Conclusion

In this book, I have explored many challenges and issues surrounding my life here in Britain as an American parent raising British children. I am raising my own children in a country and culture I myself did not grow up in and within this book I have explored the challenges that come with doing so. Furthermore, I have included the thoughts and opinions of parents from many different countries who are raising their children here in Britain. I have also given a voice to the parents who are doing what I and the parents who contributed to this book are doing. It is an emotional journey, a challenging journey, a multi-faceted journey and one that doesn't stop here. This is just the beginning of my life as an expat foreign parent to my British born, half American children, who I am raising here in Britain. In many ways I love it here and I now feel at home here. I am proud that my children are cross-cultural and will have the opportunity, should they wish, to live and work in America when they are adults. It will be interesting when they are older to see how they view themselves culturally and what aspects of their American culture they hold onto or want to explore further. Or not

Conclusion

at all, as the case might be. In other ways, at times I feel homesick, find it difficult being so far away from my own family and long for repatriation one day, which may or may not happen.

Overall, writing this book has been a passion and an achievement that I am very proud of. I hope that exploring these issues and challenges within my own family as an American mother raising British children, with a British husband, has both strengthened and given valuable insight into our cross-cultural family and other families like ours.

Appendix

**Top Ten: What we love and hate about bringing up
our children in Britain**

The following lists have been compiled from the parents
that I've interviewed. They are the top ten things we love
and hate about bringing up our children in Britain.

What we **love** - these are things we think are the main
positives and things that endear us to British culture,
specifically concerning our families and our children:

1. The NHS and free meds
2. Close proximity to European mainland
3. Free 15 hours of nursery and child benefit
4. Walking culture, great for a healthy upbringing
5. No poisonous insects or creatures like scorpions
   and black widow spiders and snakes (my eldest
   son would love it if there were poisonous insects
   in Britain)
6. British TV – Cbeebies!!
7. The wide range of baby & toddler groups and

softplay centres
8. Educational system
9. Acceptance of other cultures and races
10. Child friendly society

What we **hate** - these are things we think are challenging or frustrating specifically concerning our families and our children:

1. Lack of sun
2. Lack of open space around the houses
3. Lack of open space in general
4. Lack of outdoor lifestyle
5. The NHS and hospital care
6. Educational System
7. Initial unfriendliness of people
8. Low expectations
9. Regimented way of doing things – baby's and children's schedules, play dates and social interaction
10. Undervaluing education

Notes

1. Office for National Statistics
    Births in England and Wales by parents' country of
    birth 2009

2. *The Mumpreneur Guide: Start your own successful
    business* by Antonia Chitty
    Ac Pr 2009

3. *Notes From a Small Island* by Bill Bryson
    Black Swan 1996

4. *Dinner at The Homesick Restaurant* by Anne Tyler
    Ballantine Books Inc 1996

5. *Battle Hymn of the Tiger Mother* by Amy Chua
    Bloomsbury Publishing Plc 2011

6. *Third Culture Kids - Growing Up Among Worlds* by
    David C. Pollock and Ruth E. Van Reken
    Nicholas Brealey Publishing 2009

Resources

Publications

- *Raising Bilingual Children: Parent's Guide series* by Carey Myles

- *The Bilingual Family: A Handbook for Parents* by Edith Harding-Esch and Philip Riley

- *Divided by a Common Language: A Guide to British and American English* by Christopher Davies

- *Bum Bags and Fanny Packs: A British-American American-British Dictionary* by Jeremy Smith

- *Raising Global Nomads: Parenting Abroad in an On-Demand World* by Robin Pascoe

- *Watching the English: The Hidden Rules of English Behaviour* by Kate Fox

Resources

Useful websites

Bilingual story books, picture books and language resources for children aged 0-14years

- www.mothertonguebooks.co.uk

Find your local baby and toddler group on netmums

- www.netmums.com

NCT baby and toddler groups and NCT antenatal classes

- www.nct.org.uk

Baby & Toddler Group listings in Nottingham, Worthing & West Sussex and Brighton & Hove

- www.betterdaysout.co.uk

Online forum for mothers where you can search for helpful information or advice

- www.mumsnet.co.uk

Getting set up with Skype

- www.skype.com

Social networks photo websites – share family photos and connect internationally

- www.facebook.com
- www.kodakgallery.co.uk
- www.snapfish.co.uk
- www.photobucket.com

Resources

- www.myphotoalbum.com
- www.phanfare.com

American food products
- www.americanfooddirect.com
- www.skyco.uk.com

Middle Eastern food products
- www.aldoukan.com

Asian food products
- www.theasiancookshop.co.uk
- www.wingyipstore.co.uk
- www.thai-food-online.co.uk
- www.natco-online.com
- www.thaishopping.co.uk

Japanese sweets
- www.an-an.co.uk (Suitable for Vegetarians, Vegans. Gluten and wheat free)

Website for Americans living in the UK
- www.uk-yankee.com

Online forum for American expats
- www.americanexpats.co.uk

Resources

Online forum for expats
- www.expatforum.com

News, statistics, and information on living in the UK
- www.foreignersinuk.co.uk

The American's guide to speaking British
- www.effingpot.com

British English – American Dictionary
- www.bg-map.com/us-uk.html

For parents seeking information related to questions about raising children bilingually
- www.raising-bilingual-children.com

Multilingual Family in the UK: Find out about other parents speaking the same language as you in the area where you live
- www.multilingualfamily.org.uk

For more resources, please visit
- **www.bringingupbrits.co.uk**

About the Author

Meghan Peterson Fenn is an American expat and mother who has lived in England since 1999.

After graduating from university with a BA in English and Art, she became an English teacher and lived and worked in Prague for two years and then in Tokyo for two and a half years. She moved to England to complete her Masters degree in Design Studies and then worked as a web designer at a company in Nottinghamshire.

After being made redundant whilst pregnant with her 2nd child, she set up her own web and graphic design business, White Ochre Design. Alongside her successful business she also runs an informational website for parents, carers and grandparents of young children called Better Days Out. In addition, Meghan is the Worthing manager for The Mumpreneurs Networking Club, a group run by mumpreneurs which supports mums in business by providing a network specifically for them. She currently lives on the Southeast coast of England, is married to an English man and has 3 children, all born in the UK.

To get in touch with Meg please email her directly at:

meg@bringingupbrits.co.uk

For more information please visit:

www.bringingupbrits.co.uk

Photo by Mi Bewick Photography

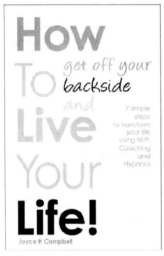

Do you feel stuck in a rut?

Are you asking yourself 'Is this IT?'

Do you see life passing you by?

Then you need this book! It's the next best thing to having your own life coach on tap 24/7!

Available from Amazon & all good bookshops

In 7 simple steps you will discover how to:

- Become 100% committed to making the changes you want

- Build the perfect support team around you

- Learn from the past and then let it go once and for all

- Appreciate the joy of living authentically in the present

- Create the fabulous future you've been dreaming about

- Keep moving forward by taking consistent action

- Stay on track for the rest of your life

'**A very useful guide for those wishing to take control of their lives and themselves.**' David R Hamilton PhD: author of *Why Kindness is Good for You*

'**This is a very friendly, easy to follow and practical book that will teach you how to successfully coach yourself to achieve the life you want. I love Joyce's 'no-nonsense' approach – it is refreshing, motivational and life changing.**' Murielle Maupoint: author of *The Essential NLP Practitioner's Handbook: How to Succeed as an NLP Therapist & Coach*